The Ten
Commandments
from the
Back Side

The Ten Commandments from the Back Side

J. ELLSWORTH KALAS

Abingdon Press
NASHVILLE

THE TEN COMMANDMENTS FROM THE BACK SIDE

Copyright © 1998 by Abingdon Press

This book is printed on acid-free paper.

Library of Congress Cataloging-in-Publication Data

Kalas, J. Ellsworth, 1923–
    The Ten commandments from the back side / J. Ellsworth Kalas.
    p. cm.
    ISBN 0-687-00524-8 (alk. paper)
    1. Ten commandments.   I. Title.
  BV4656.K35   1998
  241.5'2–dc21   97-35075
                                                                         CIP

Study guide prepared by John D. Schroeder.

98 99 00 01 02 03 04 05 06 07—10 9 8 7 6 5 4 3 2

MANUFACTURED IN THE UNITED STATES OF AMERICA

To acknowledge with gratitude two debts
I can no longer pay in person:

Hulda Weintz
my sixth grade Sunday school teacher

Bill Rhyand
unselfish friend

CONTENTS

Contents

The No That Gives Us Yes

I hope you'll understand, as you read this book, that I'm not intending to improve on the Ten Commandments. I know better than that! But I would like to improve on our understanding of these commandments, and in order to do that, I have to approach them from the back side. The ten commandments suffer from familiarity. We know them so well that we hardly know them at all.

Especially, the commandments suffer from a bad press. Someone has convinced us that God imposed these laws on us in order to keep us from enjoying life.

Not at all! In fact, the ten commandments are the gift of a loving God. They are intended to make the road of life smoother, the journey less complicated, the destination more certain. As such, they may be our best friends.

Now, of course, when I use the term "friend" in this way, I'm extending the meaning of friendship. But you're familiar with my usage. A man says as he pulls on a weatherbeaten coat, "This coat is the best friend I've ever had," and we understand that it has served him faithfully, perhaps almost to the point of saving his life. I saw a woman pushing a sturdy container into an oven. "That has seen a lot of service," I said. "Next to my husband, it's my best friend," she answered, "and sometimes he probably comes in second."

It's true that a coat, a dish, a car, a house cannot respond to us as human—or even animal—friends can; nor can the ten commandments. But all can be friends for the comfort or strength they bring into life. And none more so than those ten rather terse orders we call the Decalogue, the ten commandments.

A long-ago poet saw this clearly. He was so excited about the beauty he had found in God's law that his poem catches us unaware. He begins with words that would make us want to sing even if a composer hadn't given us a framework for doing so: "The heavens are telling the glory of God" (Psalm 19:1). And we agree readily when he says of the beauty of the heavens that "their voice goes out through all the earth" (19:4). When he tells us that the sun is like a strong man who can hardly wait to begin the day's race, his figure of speech catches us up in his excitement.

But we're caught off guard when the writer, without a transition sentence or a change of pace, continues:

> The law of the LORD is perfect,
>   reviving the soul;
> the decrees of the LORD are sure,
>   making wise the simple;
> the precepts of the LORD are right,
>   rejoicing the heart;
> the commandment of the LORD is clear,
>   enlightening the eyes. (Psalm 19:7-8)

It is soon clear that when the poet has switched, with unabated enthusiasm, from the glory of the heavens to the wonder of the Law, he hasn't done so by chance. He thinks it's appropriate to speak of these very diverse themes with the same level of ecstasy. In fact, the writer seems to suggest that the law is more wonderful than the sun, moon, or stars, because he devotes more lines to telling its story. It's as if you looked up into the sky while walking with a friend on a brilliant spring day, and said, while shading your eyes, "Isn't the sun magnificent?" And your friend answered, "Yes—and I love that stop sign, too."

The psalmist's words are so incongruous that they seem almost indecent. But the simple fact is this, that this long-ago believer was reflecting on his own experience. When he looked up into the heavens, the stars by night and the sun by day made his heart overflow with praise to God; then, when he opened the Scriptures and read the law of the Lord, he had the same wonderful sensation, only—it seems—more so. When he looked at the heavens, his heart said, "Only God could have done something as wonderful as this!"—and when he looked at the law, again his heart said, "Only God could have done anything as wonderful as this."

This isn't the only time the ancient Hebrew poets expressed such a sentiment. In fact, the longest chapter in the Bible, Psalm 119, dedicates all of its 176 verses to praising the law. It does so with a rather intricate acrostical poem, in which the writer (or writers) goes methodically through the twenty-two letters of the Hebrew alphabet, beginning each unit of eight verses with a given letter. But always, through the nearly two hundred verses, there is the same theme, the law. Sometimes the writers are giving thanksgiving for the protection the law has provided; at other times they pray that they will be more attentive to its instructions; and yet again they want nothing more than to stand back in astonishment at its inherent beauty. But always, their theme is the law, and they hold to this theme with a faithfulness that can easily become tedious to a modern reader, unless we catch the enthusiasm of the original writer.

At one point the poet is so carried away that he says,

At midnight I rise to praise you,
because of your righteous ordinances. (Psalm 119:62)

Get up at midnight to sing of the beauty of the Law? Rise out of the first hours of a sound sleep for *that*? In the cynical manner of our times we're likely to reason that the writer has some ulterior motive—that he professes to love the law only because it gives him some benefit. A lawyer might feel this way. A judge might have an additional motive: the prestige which comes to those who administer the law. Or we might recall the image of the lead professor in *Paper Chase,* and agree that a teacher of the law could also be one who loves it. If a person has no such ulterior gain yet considers the law lovable, however, we conclude that this person is probably something of a masochist, perhaps the kind of person whose hobby is cleaning stables.

After all, the business of the law is to say *no,* and nobody really likes to be told *no.* So how could anyone love the law, the very instrument of negation? The law is a stop sign, a restriction, a no-no. The law is something that interrupts just when we're winning, calls out "Foul!" and lays a penalty on us. Sometimes it calls back our touchdowns at the moment of our celebrating. How could someone sing ecstatically about laws, even to the point of putting them in the same category as the beauties of nature?

Quite simply, because these persons had discovered, again and again, over a lifetime, that the law made life better. As the one writer said, "Those who obey them are happy" (Psalm 19:8 GNB). If we had asked him to tell us what he meant, he might have answered, "I've always wanted something which would make life hold together. Make sense, you know. So many things don't. But God's law works. In a world where we search for so long for something that works, I've found it. God's law."

Different people say this in different ways. I remember the words of a mountain woman who first learned to read when she reached her mid-forties, and who was trying to analyze how, in spite of everything, she had come at last to that achievement. Raised in poverty in the mountains of Kentucky, she recalled what it was like to grow up in such a world. "When we were coming up, the next-door neighbor could spank you. It's nice to have someone to tell you right from wrong. But I didn't see that when I was young. I am thinking about it as I get older." Not only is it "nice to have someone to tell you right from wrong," as she said with simple eloquence, it is absolutely essential if we are to survive, if we are to make life "work."

For several years the church I pastored in Madison, Wisconsin, had a weekend in May in which we celebrated the artwork and handicrafts of our members. We intended by this celebration to thank God for whatever talents we might have, and to let others enjoy them as well. The displays were wonderful in their variety, and in many instances, for their excellence. They ranged all the way from a child's poems to oil paintings, from needlepoint to sculpture to pottery to woodwork.

One year a mechanical engineer in our congregation brought an intricate model to show how he had devised an artificial heart valve. His device was already being used by surgeons and was already saving lives. But his display—a confusing collection of pipes and parts—made no sense to me, and it certainly wasn't beautiful!

Then the light dawned on my rather dull mind. The beauty of the gadget was that it *worked*. It had led the way to a funny little object that was now saving lives. With that realization, I could just imagine someone who was living because of this valve; they might well stand at the collection of pipes and pulleys and say, "Beautiful! Absolutely beautiful! I've never seen anything lovelier."

I think that's the way the long-ago poet felt as he looked at the law of God. His pagan neighbors saw it as a frustrating collection of pipes and gadgets that seemed intended to take all the fun out of life. But the devout poet had discovered that the law was a lamp to his feet, an instrument to keep him from stumbling in his perilous walk through life. Yes, and more; it was his best provision for finding a lifestyle that would bring a special measure of health and fulfillment. No wonder he spoke of it in the same breath, and with the same enthusiasm, as of the sun and the stars!

Lest you think that perhaps the several poets who praised the law in their psalms were only seeking divine favor, remember what a candid and sometimes crusty company these psalmists were. If ever any body of writers felt free to speak their minds, with neither fear nor reluctance, it was that collection of persons who gave us the Psalms. If they were angry with God, they said so. If they were disappointed in the working-out of Providence, they announced it. If they thought others were getting a better deal than they deserved, they registered their complaints explicitly and angrily. Don't think they would praise the Law if they didn't mean it. You'll find no cloying sweetness in these writers. What they felt is what we get.

Those psalmists and prophets who praised the law understood what many others have not, that the law was based on love—"God's electing love for Israel," as Peter Craigie and David Jeffrey have put it (*A Dictionary of Biblical Tradition in English Literature,* 755). They recognized that God had given the law to bless, not to frustrate. The walls that the law erected were intended, not to prevent our traveling into fields of pleasure, but to prevent pain and destruction from getting at us.

When Jesus and Paul talked about the law, they made the point even clearer. Jesus insisted that he had come to fulfill the law, not to destroy it, and he did so by adding vast new areas of spiritual application. Those who thought the commandments against murder and adultery referred only to physical acts must have been startled when Jesus enlarged the definition to include anger and lust. But just as Jesus made the definitions both broader and more inclusive, he also demonstrated even more emphatically that the law was meant to make life richer and more fulfilling.

Paul added another dimension. He acknowledged that no one can fulfill all the law's demands—not if one takes the law seriously. But that's good, because in revealing our shortcomings, the law prepares us to accept grace. If we had no standard by which to measure our thoughts and conduct, we would have no idea what we ought to be, and therefore no idea of our need for redeeming grace. It would be as if the concept of beauty had never entered our lives, in which case we wouldn't be able to distinguish between excellence and ugliness, and surely not between excellence and mediocrity. So the law has defined and refined our moral taste and given us an appetite for divine excellence. And Jesus Christ, Paul explains, gives us the ability to take hold of that excellence.

Such a friend is the Law. Whether in its basic form in the Hebrew Scriptures, or in its extended and fulfilled form in the teachings of Jesus and Paul, it is our dear friend. Most of its declarations come to us in negative form, but it enlarges the possibilities for a positive life. It is the *no* which opens up the true and full potential of life's *yes*.

Are the ten commandments our friends? The very best!

CHAPTER 1

To Begin at the Beginning

....

EXODUS 20:3: You shall have no other gods before me.

God shall have all of you.

The biggest issue in life is priorities.

You don't have to be religious to know that. We all acknowledge it every day, dozens of times a day. It is the essence of life for us list-makers; we draw up the list of the things we plan to do, then start numbering them in order of priority. Those whose budget is stretched to the limits stack up their bills according to the priority rule, "Which creditor will be most heartless?" For some it gets no more existential than a box of chocolates: Do I eat the creams first, or the caramels?

Most of us manage our priorities reasonably well at these levels. Interestingly enough, we also do pretty well at the frightening extremities of life. If our house catches fire, for instance, we'll probably decide quickly and incisively about what to carry out and what to leave behind.

But life itself is a more complicated call. Renowned preacher and author George Buttrick came one day upon a farmer who had just retrieved a lost sheep. When Buttrick asked how sheep wander away, the farmer answered, "They just nibble themselves lost." They go, he explained, from one tuft of grass to another, until at last they've lost their way. And that, of course, is what happens with life. Unless we purposely establish a structure of priorities, we will nibble away at each inconsequential tuft of decision until life is gone, and we have little idea of what has happened to it.

It would be so much easier and better if life's ultimate priorities could be established in some climactic moment. That happens to some people. In wartime they call it a "foxhole experience"—the kind of situation in which life is stripped to its most elemental essentials, and we know what matters most. That's how World War II gave birth to Chaplain Cummings' truism, "There are no atheists in the foxholes." Paul Johnson, the journalist and historian, says that in times of chronic pain or of distress without apparent end, even the confirmed atheist hopes there is a God. Foxhole decisions, of whatever dimension, don't necessarily hold after the crisis is past, but at least the person can always remember that once there was a time when he or she looked all of life in the eye and recognized the absolute priority.

Almost inevitably, of course, that priority is God—and if not directly God, some factor of life in which the fruit of a God-encounter is expressed. In a sense, *Priority* is another name for God. When we draw up our little list of the things that matter most, that which we designate Number One is god. Whether or not it is God with a capital G is another matter. But by pragmatic decision, the priority which tops your list or mine will become a capital P because it will be our god. It is our governing principle, because, whether we like it or not, we become like the god (or gods) we worship. As a great preacher from earlier in this century, F. W. Gunsaulus, said, our melody of life, if it is a melody at all, "must begin yonder in the skies." Some students of world religions say that people make gods in their own images. If so, the gods—whatever they may be—return the favor. We become like what we worship. Those of us who wish we were better have probably wished that godliness came more quickly, but there can be no doubt about the method. Godliness comes from exposure—*time* exposure!—whatever the god we choose.

Not only do we become like the god we worship, but we also allow this god to determine what kind of world we will have, what kind of government we will choose, what sorts of persons we will want to rule over us; this god determines how we will choose our work, how we will feel about it, and what we will think of our bodies. And, of course, it determines what we think of people and of friendships and of human relationships. If my god is cheap, shoddy, and manageable, I will treat people the same way—all of which may raise questions about who we profess is our God, and who or what it is that we actually worship. To put it more directly, sometimes we *profess* to worship the God who is revealed in Jesus Christ, but we *demonstrate,* by our conduct, that we have quite another god.

But the point remains the same. We become like what we worship. That's why the ten commandments begin with our relationship to God. We wouldn't prioritize them that way, of course. Ask the average person for the most important commandment, and he or she will likely choose the one forbidding murder, or adultery, or dishonesty. But these commandments are all derivative; they have no point of issue except as we settle the first commandment, the matter of God. The matter, that is, of our Priority.

So the commandments begin with God, not because the commandments are religious, but because we are. They begin with God because what we think about God will eventually determine what we think of ourselves, of one another, and of life. And this means that all the other commandments rest upon this one. No wonder, then, that when a thoughtful interrogator asked Jesus to name the most important commandment, Jesus answered, "Hear, O Israel: the Lord our God, the Lord is one; you shall love the Lord your God with all your heart, and with all your soul, and with all your mind, and with all your strength" (Mark 12:29-30). Then, with convicting logic, Jesus continued, "The second [which the questioner hadn't requested] is this, 'You shall love your neighbor as yourself' " (Mark 12:31). If one accepts, *really* accepts, Jesus' first statement, he or she cannot escape the second. To love God is to be like God, and to be like God is to love our neighbor.

Jesus was quoting Deuteronomy, which is a second, expanded statement of the Law. Two words stand out: *one* and *love*. The Lord our God is *one*. Our culture speaks often about split personalities, but in this respect we are not different from any of our predecessor generations; we human creatures are always split unless we find an ultimate focus—that is, unless we find God, and focus upon God.

And *love*. We think it an unlikely word for a commandment, but that's largely because we usually think of love in an emotional sense. Love is also a state of mind, a directing of attention and of intention. In his study of Hebrew words, Benjamin Blech urges that we should use the word "love" in the sense the Hebrew root implies: "I will give." Then, he says, the love test is simple: Do I want to do more for him or her than I want him or her to do for me?

This means an ultimate kind of giving. Call it an obsession—a magnificent obsession, if it be centered on God; a divine obsession. If God be God, he should have all that we are. That is not only the essence of this first commandment; it also is its beauty and its glory. *God shall have all of you.* Of course; what else would we dare offer to God? If God is the subject of the sentence, dare anything partial be its object?

Now the truth is this: You and I want to be consumed by something. We want inherently to be possessed. Earlier in this century prize-winning poet Edna St. Vincent Millay put it graphically:

> My candle burns at both ends;
> It will not last the night;
> But, ah, my foes, and, oh, my friends—
> It gives a lovely light.
> (*A Few Figs from Thistles*)

Something in us wants to live grandly, to give ourselves with abandonment.

If we are to be consumed, if it is our very nature to seek to be consumed, we had better choose passionately as to who or what will consume us, because you and I are of such sublime importance. I am especially important to me, because I'm the only one that I have. After I have used up me, I have nothing left. I had better be sure that I choose wisely when I give myself up to a grand obsession.

Come to think of it, even if God should have me, why should it be *all* of me? Wouldn't it be better if I parceled out my substance—if I would give God some of my devotion, and give some to sex and success and baseball and collecting match-books?

Well, in truth, that's how life is frittered away. We give it up in little pieces, some of them sad absurdities, and none of them worth mentioning in the same breath with God. If life has hundreds of points, it becomes pointless. If our lives are to have a piercing quality, they will need to have a single point, a classic directness.

Three centuries ago the English poet and cleric Robert Herrick made a dramatic statement of God's claim for our all:

> God will have all, or none, serve Him, or fall
> Down before Baal, Bel, or Belial:
> Either be hot, or cold; God doth despise,
> Abhor, and spew out all Neutralities.

I wonder how and when Herrick came to that realization? He didn't always think that way. Not when he wrote, "Gather ye rosebuds while ye may," nor when he wrote

> I do love I know not what;
> Sometimes this, and sometimes that.

Before his ordination, Herrick spent much of his time with London's wittiest society, and for several years after his ordination he returned to that quite superficial culture. When did he conclude that God would "spew out all Neutralities"? Or did he struggle all his days to cope with God's demands? If I understand human nature, I venture that there was always something of such a struggle within him. But I'm also certain that—if he took his own words seriously—he came more and more to know that nothing mattered so much as to center his ultimate commitments on God—God, who demands all of us.

I hope that Herrick came to realize, as you and I should, that God's jealousy toward us is a product of God's love for us. God demands all because we are never fulfilled until we give all to him. I think of Augustine's trenchant words: "Thou hast created us for thyself, and our heart cannot be quieted till it may find repose in thee." Although Augustine was a philosopher, he wrote those words not from a position of detached speculation, but out of his experience as a person who had once been driven by the claims of both sex and success. He knew that it is our nature to have a grand passion; but unless that passion finds itself in God, it will not be satisfied.

What a measure of what we are! We declare our worth by what we worship. Is it money? If so, what a paltry price we put on ourselves! Is it physical gratification? To settle for such is to say that there is no more to us than our blood and guts and glands. What about the aesthetic—to give ourselves to beauty? In my own prejudices, this moves us higher, but it isn't high enough, because wonderful as the aesthetic is, it is a cramping, limiting measure for creatures like you and me. It is only a variation on the ancient peoples who made graven images and bowed down to them.

What, then, of family and friendship and great loyalties—to school or village or country? Surely these are high callings. Few things seem nobler than the person who will die for his or her country or child or friend. Indeed. But still, these are not *ultimates*. Beautiful as is such a devotion, it doesn't fit the greatness of our capacity. Such devotion is magnificent as an expression of our higher calling, but it is not enough to be our calling. Let God have all, then from that all, give to the persons, the values, the causes that we cherish. But let them be a result of the end, not the end in itself.

If we give ourselves to anything less than God, we underestimate ourselves. The writer of Genesis said that we human creatures are made of the dust of the earth, but that we are inhabited by the breath of God. How pathetic, how absurd, for eternal creatures like you and me to pour ourselves into embracing that which is transient! It is like a bewildered mother who lays her baby aside in order to clutch at a rag doll. Grandeur such as God has invested in us is demeaned if we give its ultimate devotion to anything less than the divine.

Mind you, giving ourselves to God in such absolute fashion will not diminish our capacity for persons or causes or aesthetics, or even that which we call "fun." To the contrary, we are better equipped to engage ourselves with the harmonies of life when we have found the supreme chord. We are more able to become involved in friendship and love, in creativity and grand doing, if our basic commitment is in order. To love God is not to love life less, but to grasp it with a surer hand, a more sensitive one. With God at the center of our life and vision, we can see more clearly what is good and beautiful in all the rest of life. With God at the center, we are most surely what we are really meant to be.

But this is not the end of the matter. The more we give ourselves to God, the more we become like God. The more of us that God has, the more we have of God. This is the nature of relationships: If I would have more of you, I must give you more of me. What is true of our human relationships is even more magnificently true of our relationship with God.

When I speak of such godliness, I do so with some uneasiness, because I'm afraid I might lose your attention. You may be inclined, on the one hand, to turn off your personal perceptions because you're sure that I'm speaking of something quite out of your reach. Believe me, I could hardly do such a thing, because in that case it would be out of my reach, too, since I'm so much like you. On the other hand, you may not hear me well because in your mind you have a picture of someone you've been told is godly and who seems to you only to be odd or unpleasantly pious.

I'm sure that the most godly people I've known have also been the most likable. They have a great excitement about living; and how could it be otherwise if one sees God at work everywhere? With such a viewpoint, life can hardly be dull. They also have a remarkable ability to roll with the punches, so that whatever happens to them, they find beauty and purpose in it. Of course, they do, because when we fix our vision on God, we are sublimely confident that a divine purpose underlies all that is happening, and that no matter what persons or circumstances may do to us, or what we do to ourselves, God will work with us to ultimate good.

The godly people I've known have also been the most admirable. In a culture that manufactures its heroes in public relations offices and measures achievements by lines in print or by television sound bites, it's exciting to find people who evoke our admiration without the aid of a press release. The delightful modern poet Phyllis McGinley says that virtue is humanity's Mount Everest, and that those who climb highest are worth admiring. Indeed so, and more than that, they are worth emulating. So to continue McGinley's figure of speech, if one is going to climb Everest, one must be committed to the project. Everest is more than an afternoon's stroll!

But godliness is not so nearly singular an adventure as is Everest. I have met godly people in literally hundreds of places, and in innumerable ages, shapes, sizes, and situations. They may be male or female, young or old, rich or poor; they are to be found in every racial and ethnic category, and in cities and open country. But one thing they have in common: God is the ultimate issue of their lives. God is their priority.

Herein is the genius of the first commandment. Life must have a focus. If we live scattershot, we will hit nothing of consequence. But, of course, focus is not enough; the focus must be *right,* else we will invest our extraordinary potential in that which is, at best, trivial, and at worst, demonic.

The first commandment reminds us, by implication, that we are creatures of eternal worth—of so much worth, in fact, that we are capable of doing business with the Lord God. If that isn't breathtaking enough, the commandment insists that God desires our attention, because God (who made us) knows how great our potential is, and how tragic it is if we invest such potential in anything less than the divine. So God gives us a commandment, that we shall have no other gods before him—not because God wishes to fence us in, but because he wishes to set us free, to give us opportunity to fulfill the capacity of our wondrous ordaining.

God shall have all of you. And you, in turn, shall be given yourself, and the wonder of fullness in God.

CHAPTER 2

Believing Is More Than Seeing

....

EXODUS 20:4: You shall not make for yourself an idol, whether in the form of anything that is in heaven above, or that is on the earth beneath, or that is in the water under the earth.

You shall adore the mystery which is beyond comprehension.

N ot many people today worry about keeping the second commandment, nor do many think it has anything to say to their way of life. Like the soldier who said, after hearing his chaplain preach on the ten commandments, "Well, at least I've never made any graven images," most of us are comfortable with this commandment. It may have meant something to the Hittites, Jebusites, and some errant Israelites, but it's no issue to anyone in what we perceive to be the civilized Western world.

In these secure feelings, we may be rather astonished that it is this commandment which carries the severe warning,

> You shall not bow down to them or worship them; for I the LORD your God am a jealous God, punishing children for the iniquity of parents, to the third and the fourth generation of those who reject me, but showing steadfast love to the thousandth generation of those who love me and keep my commandments. (Exodus 20:5-6)

For a generation that wants a serviceable God and moderate expressions of religion, such vigorous language seems as out of touch with modern life as the images it forbids.

But the commandment is there, like it or not. As it happens, I like it, because I realize that it is another expression of God's great *yes* to our human race. Like all the other commandments, it is intended to expand the borders of life, not to make life smaller or less beautiful.

One thing is very sure: This commandment was fearfully serious to the pious Jews, and to the prophets who sought passionately to keep them in line. When the Israelites wandered from God, their wanderings almost always began with a graven image. As a matter of fact, Israel broke this commandment before Moses had completed delivery of the tables of stone. It was while he was receiving the commandments at Sinai that his brother Aaron and the people got together to make golden calves to take God's place; and sure enough, they were bowing down to their idols even as Moses approached with his set of divine ordinances. When Israel finally settled into the land that was to be their home—the land in which they were to live out their unique faith—it was a violation of this commandment which signaled their spiritual unfaithfulness: They were soon bowing down to Baal and Astarte (Judges 2).

The great Hebrew prophets who eventually came on the scene found this idol worship not only repugnant but also absurd. We are likely to honor the prophets for their majestic social conscience or their vision of the coming Messiah, but for them, no subject was felt more intensely than the issue of idol worship. Jeremiah spoke with nothing less than scorn as he warned God's people:

> For the customs of the peoples are false:
> a tree from the forest is cut down,
>   and worked with an ax by the hands of an artisan;
> people deck it with silver and gold;
>   they fasten it with hammer and nails
>   so that it cannot move.
> Their idols are like scarecrows in a cucumber field,
>   and they cannot speak;

they have to be carried,
    for they cannot walk.
Do not be afraid of them,
    for they cannot do evil,
    nor is it in them to do good. (Jeremiah 10:3-5)

Jeremiah was a rational man, and he was offended that the people to whom he belonged could be so irrational as to see any power in idols—poor things that "have to be carried / for they cannot walk": How can such a helpless object strike fear into anyone's heart? The prophet Isaiah felt the same combination of astonishment and contempt as a craftsman who cuts down a cedar, a cypress, or an oak (he lists several trees, as if to indicate that anything will do) and then uses half of it to make an idol and the other half for fuel to cook his food and keep himself warm. Having roasted his meat with half the wood, he bows down to the other half and asks it to save him (Isaiah 44:12-20)!

But before we become too condescending toward the idol maker's superstition, we should consider the susceptibility of the patterns of our own culture. Consider the hotels that go from floor twelve to floor fourteen because so many people won't reside on a thirteenth floor. Or watch somebody ask to be moved from the thirteenth row on a plane. Or consider the major league baseball player who has more than sixty carefully defined superstitions that he considers as significant to his batting average as his skill in anticipating a curve ball or a slider. If superstition was the chief sin of the idol worshipers, then we may be as irrational as they were.

Of course, the issue is greater than that. Superstition may, of itself, be a relatively small matter; ridiculous, perhaps, but not crucial—except, of course, for the roots from which the superstition may spring. If idols were nothing more than the absurdities the prophets described, they would not have been an issue. Mind you, the prophets were right in their description; any idol is so illogical as to beg comprehension. But this does not diminish its danger to a worshiper.

What is that danger? Simply and directly, the individual's perception of God—and nothing could be more important than that. It goes back to the first commandment: Our picture of God determines our picture of everything else. We may not realize it, because it isn't often a conscious relationship, but our picture of God determines all our other pictures. This painting, usually splashed together so erratically, establishes the whole gallery of our existence.

The danger begins in the fact that the image is something that can be seen. A little boy is drawing intently with his crayons. When his mother asks him what he is drawing, he answers, "God." "But," his mother explains, "nobody knows what God looks like." "They will," the boy answers, "when I finish my picture." This is the essence of all our idol making. When our image is finished, we will know what our God looks like. We will have a god that can be comprehended by our senses. If we have vision, we can see the outlines of our god; if hearing, we know what God's voice should sound like; if taste, find a flavor (so the restaurant critic describes a certain sauce as "divine"); if smell, we want the incense of our altar to be just right; and if all we have is touch, we trace the contours and edges of our idol. With an idol, we have a god that can be grasped by our senses. This is very appealing, because it means that our god can be fully comprehended.

Mikhail Bakhtin grew up in an utterly atheistic society during the strength of the old Soviet Union, but in time he became a passionate believer in Christ. He concluded that if a person does not believe in God, he or she will inevitably believe in an idol—something "earthly, limited." And that's the rub: the idol-god is grounded and limited.

Here is the issue in Jesus' conversation with the woman of Samaria. Her key theological question was one that grounded and limited God: Where should God be worshiped, she asked, in the mountain endorsed by her ancestors, or in Jerusalem? Jesus broke the limits. Neither the mountain nor Jerusalem mattered, Jesus said, because "God is spirit, and those who worship him must worship in spirit and truth" (John 4:24).

Now, of course, it is true that behind the stone or wood image is someone's mental image; as the late Joy Davidman said in *Smoke on the Mountain,* her essays on the ten commandments, images are actually "solid metaphors." So why should the commandment be so specific about *graven* images? Why not a broader prohibition against all perceptions of God? If our graven images come from our thoughts, as of course they do, why doesn't the commandment forbid thinking about God—or at the least, speculating about God?

I suspect that it is because physical images are so much more restrictive, so much more effective at shutting us in. Tell me about your friend, and my mind will begin drawing a picture of him, but show me your friend's picture, and my mind has no farther to go. Now in the case of your friend, that's probably a good thing, because the picture will be more accurate than my imagining, but not so with our perception of God. There is more to God—infinitely more!—than can ever be pictured, so to make an image of God is to restrict God so much that God becomes a lie.

Joy Davidman has speculated that probably the first persons who carved idols were devout. I think she may be right. That is, God is indeed the source of fruitfulness, but of course God is much more. To make God into Baal—fruitfulness—reduces God to nothing more than an object of petulant magic. But the image won't let us go any farther, because idols reduce the infinite to the finite. They destroy the power of the imagination, restricting it to what can be seen—especially to what someone else has seen. While it is important to learn from others, it is also important to perceive and experience for ourselves. But the idol virtually insists that your God can be no bigger than what the artisan perceives God to be.

Perhaps this is something of the significance in the fierce warning which comes with this commandment, that judgment will fall on succeeding generations. Idols are the sort of creatures that go from one generation to the next. They become enshrined with tradition, so that long after the original purpose of the symbol is forgotten, its power remains. Thus the idol that one generation builds controls not only the generation that made it, but also the generations that follow, at least until someone destroys the idol. No wonder, then, that when King Josiah wanted to bring Judah back to God, he began by destroying the idols (2 Kings 23:4). The idols had, in a particular way, transmitted the curse of other generations to Josiah's time.

Another question arises: If the idols were as helpless—indeed, as absurd—as the prophets declared, why did they continue to appeal to people, so that even a nation as spiritually informed as Israel or Judah would be tempted to bow down before them? The answer is quite simple: Idols are manageable, and we humans are always looking for a manageable god.

That is, we want a god who will always do our bidding. Of course this is not limited to ancient peoples or to the primitive. It may be as big an issue today, in our materialistic culture, as it has ever been in the history of our human race. I'm a sports fan. As such, I have enjoyed the opportunity to conduct chapel services for several major league baseball teams, and I have observed with interest the athletes who witness to their faith. Some of these testimonies are very admirable and edifying. But sometimes one gets the feeling that where some ancient peoples counted on their gods to increase their crops, their modern descendants expect touchdowns, home runs, and broken records.

Obviously, this problem isn't limited to athletes. A salesperson bargains with God to get a name on the dotted line; an executive aims for victory in negotiation; a parent values God for the help he or she needs in getting a teenager to qualify for college. None of these goals is evil in itself—no more so than the abundant crop the farmer in Judah sought. But when we make God nothing more than an instrument in our drive for success, we have reduced the God of the universe to a graven image. God becomes our delivery agent, essential to our comfort, but not intended to make claims upon us. Such a god is manipulated and used. It's easy to leave this kind of god for someone else if one gets a better offer elsewhere. This is why the Hebrew prophets would so often accuse their people of spiritual adultery; they were too often looking for a god that might offer greater benefits.

Is this to say that we shouldn't ask God for material matters? Not at all. Jesus modeled such asking when he included the petition for our daily bread. But that petition came after the right mood had been established: "Hallowed be your name." Our asking must always be set in the recognition that God is God. It is quite an astonishing thing that the God of the universe should be susceptible to our appeals for help—help even in trivial matters. We ought never to exploit that divine humility, yet neither must we forget that God is insistently approachable.

As surely as idols seek to make God smaller and manageable, they also make *us* smaller. Those who worship idols, the Hebrew prophets said, are like unto them. Hosea said that when the Israelites came to Baal-peor to worship the pagan idols, they "consecrated themselves to a thing of shame, / and became detestable like the thing they loved" (Hosea 9:10). If one bows again and again before the image of an ox, one begins to take on that image—not, of course, in a physical sense, but in self-perception. The ox becomes the measure of my person; after all, if I humble myself before the ox, I acknowledge that I am the ox's inferior, and that the ox possesses something I need.

Perhaps someone will remind me that it wasn't the ox itself which ancient peoples worshiped; it was the agricultural prosperity the ox or calf represented. Of course! But this doesn't make the matter any better. The novelist describes the miser as getting a complexion like the gold he adores. If we measure our lives by the abundance of our crops, or by the size of our house or car, or by the extent of our holdings, we are dismal creatures indeed. It might be better to choose the ox!

So to what kind of God would the Law have us bow down? To a God altogether beyond us, a God who is, indeed, *God!* Not six or seven feet tall, not with my particular color or pigment of hair, and surely not a god who is valuable only for what it can do for me. Anselm, the eleventh-century philosopher who became archbishop of Canterbury, said that "God is that, the greater than which cannot be conceived." Now there's a stretch for the mind! Just how would one make an image of such a God? "Impossible!" we answer; and that, of course, is the point. The God revealed in the Scriptures is beyond any image we can make, including any image of the mind.

Of course, we will make our mental images; we must, in order to have enough perception of God to establish a relationship. The Bible lays out all sorts of possibilities for us, not only in the names that it gives to God and the figures of speech describing God, but also in the pictures of God in action. We give special content to those biblical pictures by our personal experiences with God; each moment of prayer, each day of living, each experience of God's grace adds meaning to what the Bible tells us of God's character and person.

But always, God will be beyond us; and for that, we should thank God! Madeleine L'Engle, the novelist and lay theologian, says that when Athanasius, the great fourth-century defender of the faith, wrote about God, it was "as though he were trying to catch hold of the whirlwind." I sense the same wild groping for words when the apostle Paul tries to explain the grandeur of Christ and the potential of our lives in him. Where can we find words for such perceptions? At those moments when we know that our perceptions themselves are incapable of what we instinctively sense is "out there," where can we possibly find words to capture what we can't really perceive? No one is poet enough. And if we can't find words to grasp even the god-feelings that we have, let alone be able to transfer those feelings to paper, what images of stone or wood could possibly be adequate? No wonder the Law forbade making graven images, and no wonder the prophets looked with a mixture of horror and scorn when people did so. Since heaven and the heaven of heavens cannot contain God, how monstrously I will distort God if I make an image of wood or stone. And what violence I do to the character of God—and to my own possibilities of integrity—if I make God manageable, my compliant errand-runner!

Someone has said that to fill God's place with an image is like blotting the sun out of the heavens and substituting a 15-watt bulb in its place. There is so much of God to be known, so much of the divine goodness to be released in our lives, that any limiting of God is unthinkable. As Joy Davidman said, the real horror of idols is not simply that they give us nothing, but that they take away even what we have. Believing is more than seeing—even more than learning or experiencing. The second commandment sets us free to enter into more of the grandeur and majesty of God—and in the process we become more fully ourselves.

My family remembers with amusement my coming out of anesthesia after surgery. When they asked how I felt, I answered blissfully, "It's all such a mystery, such a mystery!" I have just such a feeling as I enter into the greater precincts of the wonder of God. It is such a wondrous mystery that neither I nor anyone else will ever come to its limits. How wrong it would be to dwarf it by an image!

CHAPTER *3*

Living in the Name

....

EXODUS 20:7: You shall not make wrongful use of the name of the
LORD your God, for the LORD will not acquit anyone who misuses
his name.

You shall enter into God's name.

I sometimes say, after more than forty years of baptizing
infants, that if you will tell me a person's given name, I
can identify the decade in which he or she was born. My
mother's generation had Minnie and Lena, but no Amber or
Tiffany. Names have their seasons, their periods in the sun, as
surely as other fads and enthusiasms.

Not so with people in the biblical world. Names were
chosen for more than euphony or passing popularity, and for
more than pleasing some relative. History was sometimes
written into a name, as with poor Ichabod (1 Samuel 4:21-22).
Names were sometimes changed in the course of the faith
journey, so that Abram became Abraham, Sarai became
Sarah, and Jacob became Israel. Names were important to the
Jews, and to other ancient peoples, because they were understood as encapsulating the whole person. To know someone's
name was to know their soul.

Something of this significance continues even in our more
casual age. At times we're almost frantic to get on a first-name
basis. Service and luncheon clubs insist on it; someone has
said that it was a Rotarian who first called John the Baptist
"Jack." New clergy sometimes announce on their first Sunday,

or in an introductory column in the church paper, that they want to be called by their first names. We acknowledge that names are important, and that their use can be powerful. So the telephone salesperson says, "Mrs. Smith—may I call you 'Sally'?—I'd like to talk with you about your auto insurance." Why does he or she want to call Mrs. Smith, Sally? Because by doing so he has moved into a new level of intimacy; it's harder to say no to someone who calls you by your first name than to someone who knows you only on a formal basis.

We're still hostage to names, no doubt about it. When I was a young preacher and addressed a respected older colleague as "Doctor," I felt embraced when he answered, "My friends call me Ralph." On the other hand, if you have just won a new title, you are gratified when a friend says, warmly and with a smile, "Good morning, Doctor!" or "Congratulations, Madam President!" Corporations ready to introduce a new product invest hundreds of thousands of dollars in market research and in think-tank deliberations to come up with a name which they hope will help the sale of their product. Yes, even in these days of more casual style, we acknowledge that names are important. We resist when a business or an agency seeks to reduce us to a number; that's the mark of a convict. A name has history, heritage, personality, and therefore some measure of dignity. "Just mention my name" is a phrase that suggests power all the way from the village store to the halls of Congress.

So the third commandment says, "You shall not make wrongful use of the name of the LORD your God, for the LORD will not acquit anyone who misuses his name" (Exodus 20:7). Or, in the sonorous language of the King James Version, "Thou shalt not take the name of the LORD thy God in vain; for the LORD will not hold him guiltless that taketh his name in vain."

Why? Is God defensive of his position? Is the divine akin to the person who rules out friendship with a new acquaintance because that person mispronounces her name? Is God like the person who says, "I'm not Jim to you, I'm Doctor Jones"? If God is as insecure as that, the universe has a problem, and it's bigger than nuclear destruction. There must be more to this commandment than the protection of divine rights or issues of sacred protocol.

The issue, it seems to me, is waste. The phrase of this commandment that sticks in most of our memories, "Thou shalt not take the name of the LORD thy God in vain," is to the point. God's name is powerful, more powerful than we shall ever fully perceive. Because God's name is available to us, so too is the power of that name. If we use it *in vain*—in a fashion contrary to its character, or in trivial fashion, perhaps even debasing it—then we have *wasted* it. God has been divinely generous in revealing his name, and thus in making himself available to us. What could be a greater insult to that generosity than to use the gift carelessly or crudely? That is, *in vain*. And how could we be more destructive of our own welfare than to misuse such a gift?

We misuse God's name in more ways than even the most sensitive of us will ever realize. The curse is, of course, the most dramatic misuse. Most curses are quite casual; as some anonymous wise person said in another generation, profanity is the language a person uses to fill the gaps when the brain misses fire. But some curses are serious and intended, at least for the moment of hot anger, when someone really does intend to damn (in whatever measure they perceive the term) another party.

I can't really say a good word for cursing, of course, because it is aimed at destruction, and because it so dramatically misuses God's name. Nevertheless, in a very perverse way, a curse is a tribute to the name of God. After all, no one ever curses in a trivial name, or even in a historically significant one. How interesting that no one says, "Benjamin Franklin damn you!" He may have been a notable patriot, inventor, and a national hero, but cursing is altogether out of his league. Perhaps the person who curses takes God more seriously—

even if in a perverted way—than the secularist who seems never to give a thought to God or to God's name.

But cursing, however bad it may be, is not the chief peril for most of us. We are more likely to sin by using God's name casually or inappropriately. The issue may be all the greater for those of us who are religious, because we use the name of God more often. Familiarity doesn't necessarily breed contempt, but it does breed—well, *familiarity.*

This frightened the devout ancient Jews. They feared that even when using God's name religiously, they might slip over a line into unwarranted intimacy. As a result, they came to feel that the most sacred name for God, YHWH (Yahweh), was better not used at all, except on the annual Day of Atonement, when the high priest spoke it in the Temple. They believed that the Tabernacle (Deuteronomy 12:11) and Solomon's Temple (1 Kings 8:20) were specific places where God's Name would dwell, and they were therefore cautious about using it in other circumstances and settings.

This caution has carried over to the present day in the practices of the *soferim,* the scribes who copy the Torah for the temple scrolls. They are so infused with the sacredness of their task that they work only with the skin of a kosher animal, prepared according to careful regulations, and using a formula ink. More than that, the *sofer* must go to a ritual bath before his day's work; and before beginning his copying, he recites a special prayer. Now with all of this, one would think reverence was complete. But when the *sofer* is about to copy the name of God, he pauses for another, special prayer. Such is the sense of awe with which God's name is treated.

Anyone who has made a thoughtful reading of Psalms or the prophets will see a striking incongruity in all of this. I know of no literature that is more direct in its communication with God, or more candid in outlining what it perceives to be God's shortcomings, than so many of the psalms. How fascinating that the psalmists and prophets could so insistently challenge God, yet be so circumspect in using God's name!

Why? Because God's name is God's very person, and to use God's name disrespectfully or unworthily is to treat God so. It is one thing to raise questions with God about the way the universe is run and whether certain divine judgments are fair or even, in the psalmist's mind, rational; but it is quite another to misuse God's name. The name is the essence of God's very person; to use that name casually is to treat God with contempt.

The devout found beauty and strength in God's name. "Your name and your renown," Isaiah said, "are the soul's desire" (Isaiah 26:8). A little later he confesses sadly that other lords have ruled over them, "but we acknowledge your name alone" (Isaiah 26:13). They might not be able to control who would rule over their bodies and their civic life, but they could, and would, determine the point of their final allegiance, the Name. The prophet Jeremiah, speaking in God's stead, chided the people for their misuse of the Name: "But you have abused my name, because you broke your agreement" (Jeremiah 34:16 CEV). God's Name is so much God's person that when we break our contract with God, we dishonor the Name.

We have a parallel for understanding what Jeremiah is saying. If you and I enter into a contract and make it binding by signing our names, I dishonor not only my name but also yours if I violate the contract. I show contempt for your name—and for you—by breaking the statement to which both of us have inscribed our persons.

The force of the dishonor is in the power of God's name for goodness. "The name of the God of Jacob protect you!" the psalmist prayed (Psalm 20:1). Why not simply, "May God protect you"? Because the Jews were sure that the Name itself was powerful. It was not a hocus pocus or a magic incantation—though, no doubt, for some it sometimes slipped into that; it was simply that the Name of God, when spoken devoutly, carried the authority of God.

No wonder, then, that when persons in the Old Testament were visited by God's representatives, they wanted to know their names. After Jacob had wrestled with the stranger and his own name had been changed—and wonderfully up-graded!—he wanted to know the stranger's name (Genesis 32:29). Of course! Because if he knew the name, he might be able to use it in some future time of need. So it was when an angelic visitor came to Manoah and his wife, to tell them that they would be given a son, Samson, who would lead their people. Manoah wanted to know the visitor's name, so he could honor him, but the visitor advised him, quite directly, that he didn't need to know the name, and that even if he knew it, he wouldn't understand it (Judges 13:17-18). My sympathies are with Manoah. If a stranger came to my door to tell me I had won a momentous prize, I'd want to know who he or she was. That is, I would want to know if the person had a name I could count on.

When the disciples asked Jesus to teach them to pray, Jesus began with a name for God, and then with an attitude toward the name: "Our Father in heaven, hallowed be your name" (Matthew 6:9). By giving God a relational name—indeed, a *family* name—Jesus indicated the nature of our approach to God. God is a Person and is personal; the name says so. God is not to be addressed as the end of a syllogism, but as One with whom we dare to claim relationship.

We shouldn't allow contemporary sexist discussions to rob us of that fact. There are some, and always have been some, who are troubled by the term "father," because their own family experience has cast a shadow over that title. But this problem is inherent in all of our human vocabulary; no term comes to us without some possible unfortunate associations. We need, therefore, to look beyond the particular term to see the insight back of the term. When Jesus encouraged his followers to call God "father," he gave a special claim on God's attention. We are neither strangers nor helpless suppliants; we are family members who dare to address God with the utmost intimacy.

But if anyone should presume upon that intimacy, Jesus

reminds us that God's name—whatever name we use—should be "hallowed" in our using. It is almost as if Jesus were giving us a positive version of the third commandment. We do not take God's name "in vain," we *hallow* it.

Then Jesus took his followers a step farther, and in doing so, brought God a step closer. Whatever we ask of God, Jesus said, we should ask in his name, and whatever we ask in his name, God will grant (John 16:23-24).

So much can be said about this extraordinary statement. Without a doubt, Jesus meant that we should pray in a spirit consistent with his character and will, because to speak otherwise and then add the name of Jesus would be nothing short of blasphemy. How would we dare to make un-Jesus-like prayers, then attach Jesus' name to them? To pray in Jesus' name is to assume Jesus' will and purpose.

It is also clear that Jesus intended to add to our authority in prayer. How do we approach God? Not on our own authority, but in the name of Jesus. My boyhood credentials were not great in the working-class world of the Great Depression, but when I came to the place where my father worked, I had some standing. "If you're John's boy," someone would say, "you're all right." I gained status because I came in the name of another. When we accept Jesus Christ as Lord, we gain just such credentialing—though, of course, in a far greater measure.

The first disciples learned this lesson well. If any single phrase characterizes the book of Acts, it is "in the name of Jesus," or some variation thereof. When the crowds on the Day of Pentecost asked Peter, in awe and fear, what they should do, Peter told them to be baptized in the name of Jesus Christ (Acts 2:38). When Peter and John came upon a lame man at the temple gate, they commanded his healing in the name of Jesus Christ (Acts 3:6). And when, as a result of this healing, the apostles were brought to the authorities for questioning, the first question addressed to them was, "By what power or by what name did you do this?" (Acts 4:7). Peter's answer was probably more sharp and direct than the authorities expected, for he advised them that the name of Jesus was the only name under heaven by which persons might be saved (Acts 4:12).

The apostle Paul carried the matter still farther. When he wrote to the Christians at Philippi, he broke into what many scholars believe was one of the earliest hymns of the Church, including the lines

> Therefore God also highly exalted him [Jesus]
>   and gave him the name
>   that is above every name,
> so that at the name of Jesus
>   every knee should bend.
>   (Philippians 2:9-10)

The early Christians had no doubt about the Name. It was their song, their assurance, and their life-and-death confession. When they spoke it, it was often at peril to their lives. But it was always a conquest of eternity.

Unfortunately, we seem to have lost this glory. We no longer have the grand *Yes* of the third commandment, the commandment that encourages us to live in the power of God's name. If some take God's name in vain by cursing, many others of us do so by neglecting its wonder and power.

I'm quite sure that if you and I were truly to honor God's name, we would honor the very principle of names—our own included! When I understand the power that is in the name of God, I will elevate my opinion of the name which was given to me by my parents, and by the church. It is a wondrous thing to have a name, and it ought never to be spoken apologetically—nor should it be defaced by improper living.

When I understand the power that is in the name of God, I will also be more respectful of the names I give to others. How dare I call someone by a derogatory name—nigger, kike, stupid—when God carries a name and ordains the very business of names? No wonder Jesus warns that when we call another person "Empty-head" (Raca) or "fool," we are in danger of hell (Matthew 5:22). Names are serious business, because it is by the name of God, and of Jesus Christ, that we enter into the possibilities of our faith.

But many of us, fearful that we will let our religion slip over into magic, are cautious about all that I am saying. Perhaps we have known someone who spoke all too easily of the name of Jesus; it may even have been "in vain," in the sense that they threw about the sacred name as if it were their casual possession.

I am as fearful of this possibility as anyone. As surely as many earnest people speak of God too little, some swing the pendulum to the other extreme, using the name of God as a kind of all-purpose charm. But there is a middle ground, a proper place, and we shouldn't allow an extreme to keep us from a grand reality. The scriptures and several millennia of tradition show us the extraordinary wonder of the name of God; and what is especially astonishing is that this wonder is so immediately accessible to any who dare, reverently, to enter into its possibilities.

Bede Griffiths, the Oxford-educated Benedictine monk, wrote recently, "If anyone ask me how I pray, my simple answer is that I pray the Jesus prayer." This is the ancient prayer, "Lord Jesus Christ, Son of God, have mercy on me, a sinner." That prayer, Griffiths says, has been his mainstay for more than forty years (John Wilkins, *How I Pray;* London: Dartman, Longman & Todd, 10). Madeleine L'Engle, prize-winning author and notable Episcopal laywoman, recalls in her book, *Rock That Is Higher,* that as she lay for torturous days after a near-fatal automobile accident, she repeated the Jesus Prayer literally thousands of times. She had neither the energy nor the will to say more, but these words sustained her.

More than a century ago, Lydia Baxter and William Doane put this love for the name of Jesus into a hymn. Simple as it is, it continues to be used in both public and private worship to this present time: "Take the name of Jesus with you, / child of sorrow and of woe; / it will joy and comfort give you; / take it then, where'er you go"; and then, a refrain that says simply, "Precious name, O how sweet!" The style of the hymn is quite different from the stark directness of the third command- ment, but the sense of reverence for the name of God is the same. It is simply stated positively.

John Milton, at times the most eloquent and perceptive commentator on Scripture, imagines in *Paradise Lost* a scene at the naming of the animals (Genesis 2:19-20). Adam asks God by what name he may address God, who "surpassest far my naming," so that he may rightly adore him. In Milton's account, Adam's question is left unanswered.

But in truth, wonder of grace, we *are* given a Name; indeed, several. And with those names, we enter into some measure of the dignity, the majesty, the beauty, and the power of the One named. This is why the Name should never be wasted, whether by profane or casual use, or by dreadful neglect. The third commandment is God's grand *Yes*—the divine invitation to enter into the name of God, and of our Savior, Jesus Christ.

CHAPTER 4

The Gift of Rest

....

EXODUS 20:8-10a: Remember the sabbath day, and keep it holy. Six days you shall labor and do all your work. But the seventh day is a sabbath to the LORD your God.

The sabbath will keep you.

As I watched my son and daughter-in-law putting their two-year-old to sleep, I saw the sabbath issue in new light. We humans don't know how to handle rest. We manage it a little better than a two-year-old at nap time, but not much. Yes, after a certain age we realize that we need our sleep, and we cherish the prospect of falling asleep at night. But we still don't grasp the rhythm of our bodies and minds; we don't understand that as surely as we need sleep at certain intervals, we need a day that is a break from the common run.

So it's no wonder that we have made the fourth commandment an object of controversy rather than what it is, a source of simple, exquisite blessing. Is it that we are too restless to rest? Or is it that we have difficulty recognizing a gift when it is given? How is it that we make the gift of the sabbath into a thicket of legalisms, void of both joy and rest—and then, tiring of our legalisms, cast the whole gift aside, in the proverbial "throwing out the baby with the bath water"?

Perhaps it is because our view of God is so faulty. We insist on seeing God as a demander rather than as a giver. The sabbath as gift looks too good to be true; why would God want to do something so utterly kind? So we look for some meanness in the graciousness of God, and finding none, we impose strictures of our own. We need to remember, with Frederick W. Faber, the nineteenth-century Catholic poet, that

> . . . the love of God is broader
> than the measure of our mind;
> and the heart of the Eternal
> is most wonderfully kind.

The people to whom Moses gave the commandments may have been better equipped than we are to recognize the sabbath as a gift. For centuries they had been a slave people; as such, they could have a day of rest only at the whim of those who owned them. Here was the difference between slavery and freedom: free people worked at their own discretion and desire, or by contract with an employer, but slaves worked at the command of others. The sabbath commandment gave the Israelites a new estimate of themselves—indeed, a surprising status of dignity. They, too, could enjoy the luxury of a day without demands—well, except for one demand, that they must make the day holy by their rest. But what a remarkable way to make a day holy!

Common sense says that we make something holy by our efforts and our deeds, or perhaps by our gifts. This command-ment insists, quite illogically, that we make a day holy by *resting*. At first glance, it sounds like an endorsement of sloth or laziness; it runs contrary to all the ancient rules about the early bird and the worm, the danger of idle hands, and the rewards that come to the industrious. If work is good—and this com-mandment certainly implies that it is, by its reference to six days of labor—then isn't more work still better?

But if we're inclined to downgrade this rest-command-ment, we are sharply corrected by the endorsement that is built into it. We are to have a sabbath of rest because God took such a sabbath. When we rest—in proper fashion—we are being *godly!* Imagine that! As some unknown rabbi in the medieval period said, if God, who never grows weary, rested

on the seventh day, how much more should we human creatures take rest on the sabbath from our weariness.

When you look at it that way, our workaholic patterns
smack of a kind of blasphemy; rest may be good enough for
God, but I'm above all of that. In some cases, our unwilling-
ness to take a sabbath is evidence of our feeling indispensa-
ble—the universe may survive God's taking a day of rest, but
it will fall apart if we do so! For others, it is an absence of trust;
we're sure that if we don't work seven days a week, we won't
survive economically. And in every case, we're failing to see
God's sublime goodness.

As I've said, we've had this problem for a long time. I
sometimes think the sabbath commandment wasn't more
than a week old before someone began trying to define its
boundaries. By Jesus' time, there were 1,521 things that a
person could not do on the sabbath. The Jerusalem Talmud
had 64 pages and the Babylonian Talmud 156 double pages
of specific rules dealing with the sabbath. It isn't surprising
that many of them took on the quality of the absurd. For
instance, a person with a toothache couldn't gargle with
vinegar but could use a toothbrush dipped in vinegar; a radish
could be dipped in salt, but not left too long in the salt, lest it
begin to pickle. No wonder the enemies of Jesus looked to the
sabbath laws as a way of entrapping Jesus, and no wonder Jesus
challenged what his contemporaries—and generations of
their ancestors—were doing to the gift of the sabbath.

For all the enlightenment Jesus brought to the sabbath, his
followers haven't treated it any better than did the most
legalistic of Pharisees. In seventeenth-century Scotland, a man
was thrown into jail for *smiling* on the sabbath. No wonder Joy
Davidman, the poet-essayist and wife of C. S. Lewis, said that
the bigots recast the fourth commandment to read, "Thou
shalt not enjoy life on Sunday."

If legalists destroyed the sabbath in times past, the libertari-
ans are doing so in our time. There are still pockets of legalism
in both Judaism and Christianity, but not many of us need to

fear that danger. Sunday, the Christian expression of the sabbath, has become the chief residence of commerce and sports. And it isn't just a matter of professional sports. In hundreds of communities, the Sunday school now has to compete with the Sunday morning hockey or soccer leagues of the sixth-grader, or the curling leagues of their parents and grandparents.

So what is the sabbath all about? Our answers should begin where the sabbath begins, in the Genesis story. In six days, the commandment reminds us, the Lord made heaven and earth, "and all that is in them," and then rested. But Genesis makes clear that it was not the rest of exhaustion, but of joy and fulfillment. God had surveyed the finished work and had declared it to be "very good" (Genesis 1:31). The sabbath is a celebration of tasks well done; it is the fragrance of a cake pulled from the oven, the closing of a barn door with the milking done and the cattle fed, the surgeon stepping back from the sick bed with the knowledge that disease has been held at bay. This is the joy of the sabbath; the work is done, and it is "very good." While that is not the issue of the sabbath, it is surely a factor to be honored: philosophically, the sabbath is hobbled when our work is, for one reason or another, deprived of satisfaction.

But that thought needs to be turned around and viewed from another side. In many instances, our work lacks satisfaction because we have not rested as we should. If some find it hard to rest because they haven't worked well, perhaps even more find their work wearisome and frustrating because they haven't rested well. Some workaholics are driven not so much by their love of work as by their search for fulfillment—yet fulfillment evades them because they are too exhausted to see their work in a positive light. Fatigue not only makes cowards of us all, it also makes us pessimists. Even the most beloved tasks become drudgery if we are unduly tired. We lose all ability to see our work with objectivity, let alone with optimism and thanksgiving.

The Old Testament Law required not only that people should rest on the sabbath, but also that they should give their land a sabbath every seven years. When at last the Jews were taken into captivity by Babylon, the prophet said that God was now collecting on unkept sabbaths—that the land would now lie idle for all of those years when they had violated its seventh-year rest periods. I think something like that happens to people who neglect their rest. It is not that God sends them into a Babylonian captivity; it is that their bodies, their psyches, their excitement-in-toil simply give out. This may explain persons all of us have known—perhaps even have been: the persons who seem to love their work with a passion until one day, apparently without warning, they become so disillusioned that they throw it all away. It may well be that life is collecting its unkept sabbaths.

No wonder, then, that a Jewish scholar said it was not so much that the Jews kept the sabbath as that the sabbath kept the Jews. This is the point of my reshaping of this commandment. The sabbath keeps us and blesses us when we are wise enough to give it its place.

The sabbath gives a peculiar and wonderful dignity to life. The Jews knew this, as I said earlier, because the sabbath was given to them against a backdrop of slavery. Every seven days the sabbath announced dramatically that they were a free people. And generations of Jews living in ghettos and poverty found that they could continue to escape from these peculiar forms of slavery by way of the sabbath. Here was a day of dignity. Hermann Cohen, looking back on centuries of such Jewish history, called the sabbath "the most capable patron saint of the Jewish people." Once the sabbath lamp was lit, he said, the ghetto Jew shed the toil and trouble of his day-to-day life. The love of God came with special glory on each seventh day, bringing "honor and human dignity even in his lowly hut." Judah Halevi, a learned observer with a sense of poetry, called the sabbath a queen whose arrival transformed the humblest home into a palace.

Perhaps it is ironic, but those who live in middle-class comfort need this day as badly as did the poorest ghetto inhabitants. We can so easily become mere machines, or extensions of machines. Charlie Chaplin dramatized this fact memorably a generation ago; I wonder how he would say it today, to a generation taken captive by computers, work stations, fax machines, and cellular phones? Chaplin knew only a world where the factory controlled the worker; ours is a world where the work follows the worker to the automobile, the dinner table, the party, and even the bedroom. Has ever a generation needed a sabbath as desperately as does ours? And was there ever a generation more in danger of losing its true dignity while so passionately in search of an acquired dignity?

Consider also the dignity which comes when we are delivered from the routine. Both Jeremiah (17:21-23) and Ezekiel (22:26) mourned that their people had come to treat the sabbath like any other day. Probably the prophets were thinking especially of the spiritual significance of the sabbath, but nothing is exclusively spiritual, just as nothing is ever exclusively secular; the two always intersect. A modern translation pictures Ezekiel saying that the priests "don't even teach the difference between what is sacred and what is ordinary" (Ezekiel 22:26 CEV). The words are significant: The opposite of sacred may not always be the profane; it is also sometimes the ordinary.

God created life to have its mountain peaks, its grand arenas of excitement. We are so put together that we need high days, times that are different from the routine. Such days help us to look upon ourselves with greater self-regard. Birthdays sometimes do this, of course, as do other occasional celebrations, such as Mother's Day or Labor Day. But God, in wondrous generosity, has given us a grand oasis at every seventh station, a sabbath! On that day, we are privileged—if we will—to step out of the common and the ordinary and into the special, the exalted, the grand. Noah benShea, a contemporary Jewish writer, explains this by saying that our life is like a tapestry—which means that, by its very nature, we are working at it from the back, "in a blind." The sabbath allows us, benShea says, to step back and turn the tapestry over so we can see "the larger pattern of who we are," and thus the implication of our relationship to the world in which we do our work. The sabbath delivers us not only from slavery, as it usually is defined, but also from the self-imposed slavery of those who have grown weary of work, or who have become extensions of their machines; it restores to us the dignity which ought to be inherent in work and in our basic humanity.

For many centuries the best of the Jewish teachers have seen the sabbath as a day of celebration. Worship is linked with rest and rejoicing, and holiness is wholeness. Hiyya ben Abba insisted that the sabbath was given "only for pleasure"; and he did not mean this only in a spiritual sense. "Sanctify the Sabbath with food, drink, clean garments and pleasure," he said, "and God will reward you for it!"

"Clean garments." When a vast majority of Americans worked at very physical tasks, on the farm or in the factory or home, our work clothes were common and crude, and we spoke of "dressing up in our Sunday best." Perhaps for some it was show and display, but for most of us it was a wonderful step out of ordinariness. I often ponder the difference these days when I preach to boomer and buster congregations, made up largely of professionals—people who dress up for work all week—and see that they have come to church in casual clothing. Perhaps this is their form of special garments. I have to struggle to see it that way, but perhaps it is so.

In any event, the mood of the sabbath should be one of celebration—but only after worship has had its primary place. As the Talmud said, "Devote part of the Sabbath to Torah [the study of the Jewish Law], and part to feasting." And rest, of course; as Yalkut Reubeni, a seventeenth-century rabbi said, "Sleep on the Sabbath is a pleasure." One Jewish scholar also insisted, "Tell nothing on the Sabbath which will draw tears."

How wise! It is possible to refrain from all physical labor yet exhaust ourselves with emotional distress. I submit that it is as wicked to fret, regret, and resent on the sabbath as to sweat over dollars. The psyche needs rest as badly as the body; perhaps more so.

One of the finest Jewish scholars of this century, Abraham Joshua Heschel, makes much of the fact that the sabbath demonstrates the holiness of time. He reminds us that time was hallowed by God—at the instituting of the sabbath at the close of creation—before any *place* was declared holy. Six days a week, Heschel says, we "live under the tyranny of things of space"; on the sabbath we try to regain this sense of holiness in time. We see time as sacred for its own sake, rather than for what we can accomplish within its boundaries. Time is God's essential gift to our human race; without it, no other gift is possible. By proper use of the sabbath, we thank God for the gift of time. And in a world which is so absorbed with *space*—with land, buildings, shopping malls, stadiums, even church buildings, and with the acquisition of such "space"—the sabbath reminds us that time deserves our primary attention, because time is the first element of our creation that God identified as being sacred. Space clamors insistently to take over our lives. The sabbath wards it off every seventh day, in the name of time.

But how shall we celebrate the sabbath rightly? I can't improve on the words of Jesus. He was so often challenged by the legalists of his day—most of them sincere men, anxious to protect the law as they understood it—because he didn't observe the sabbath in their rigid fashion. Jesus explained, "The sabbath was made for humankind, and not humankind for the sabbath" (Mark 2:27). This day is God's gift to our human race, a jewel fashioned by a loving Lord. It is holy by nature; we are privileged to keep it holy by the manner in which we enjoy it.

The manner has more to do with our attitude than with the particulars of our conduct. As I look at the history of both

Judaism and Christianity, I am convinced that those "particulars" may be the greatest enemy of the true hallowing of the day, because the particulars always squeeze out the spirit by defining the boundaries. Shall I walk? If so, how far? Shall I play? If so, how much? We want to fence off the sabbath, so that we can say, "I have kept it." But the sabbath is a gift, and the proper response to a gift is to love it.

Some of our faith ancestors lost the sabbath in legalisms; we are losing it in oblivion—we don't even know it is an issue. But however one loses it, the loss is monumental. It is not simply that we have violated God's law, but that we are frustrating God's kindness. And with it all, we are the losers, because the sabbath keeps us. It protects us from self-destruction.

Say this to all the workaholics, who think creation will collapse unless they stay on the job. And say it to all the bottom-line fanatics, who think life is measured by the things they will, by their working, get. And say it, especially, to those who set out frantically every Friday night to "relax" in a mad rush of activities. Say: "Here is God's gift, a piece of sacred time in a world of grasping space. Embrace it, and thank God for it. Adore God for thinking of our human race with such love as to give us such a gift. Smile, because this is the loveliest, happiest day of all the week. And don't worry so much about the particulars of how you keep this day; instead, rejoice in the One who has given it. If you do, the Sabbath will keep you."

CHAPTER 5

Futures Unlimited

....

EXODUS 20:12: Honor your father and your mother, so that your days may be long in the land that the LORD your God is giving you.

You shall accept the blessing of the past
so you can have a future.

Whenever word came to my childhood home of some aged parent who was in dire financial circumstances, my mother would respond with one of her favorite bits of folk wisdom: "One mother can raise five children, but five children can't take care of one mother." She was reflecting, even if somewhat cynically, the ancient belief that children are the ordained means of economic security for their parents. For untold centuries—and still today in the developing nations—peoples have seen large families as a blessing, because when the parents grow old, these children will be their providers. No wonder the psalmist said,

> Like arrows in the hand of a warrior
> are the sons of one's youth.
> Happy is the man who has
> his quiver full of them.
> (Psalm 127:4-5)

The fifth commandment does not by any means deny that honored assumption, but it does turn it around for another viewing. It reminds children that when they care for their parents—"honor" them is a wonderfully inclusive word—they are really caring for themselves.

The Brothers Grimm put that truth in a rather stinging fairy tale. Once there was a little old man, of trembling hands and feeble eyes, whose uncertain table habits became increasingly offensive to the daughter-in-law with whom he lived, until one day she objected vigorously to her husband, the old man's son. She and her husband took the fumbling old man to a corner of the kitchen, set him on a stool, and gave him his food in an earthenware bowl. Now he was no longer troubling them by his dribbled food; now the tablecloth was no longer soiled by his trembling behavior.

One day, in his trembling, he dropped the bowl and broke it. Now the daughter-in-law ceased even her moderate civility. "If you are a pig," she said, "you must eat from a trough." And they made a little wooden trough, and he ate from it.

The pride of their lives was their own four-year-old son. One evening they noticed the boy playing with blocks of wood in the serious fashion which children so often invest in their play. When the father asked what he was doing, the boy said with an engaging smile, "I'm making a trough to feed you and Mamma out of when I get big."

For a while the man and woman just looked at each other, not saying anything. Then they cried; and then they went to the corner and led the little old man back to his place at the table. They gave him a comfortable chair, and put his food on a plate. And never again were they really, deeply troubled by the food he spilled or by the dishes he occasionally broke. They had learned that, in honoring a parent, they possessed their own future.

In many ways, the world that first received the ten commandments was very different from our own. Theirs was an agricultural economy, and it was family agriculture, with the whole family working together for the common need. It wasn't necessary to plan for family time; in truth, there was very little time that wasn't family time. It would be hard to identify anything like our modern social agencies, which seem often to supplement family operations; and while government existed, it rarely dared intrude upon the distinctive prerogatives of the family.

But we live in an urban culture, where children are often lucky if they see their parents at one meal a day. Nearly all children beyond a certain grade have their lunch at school, and now several million have their breakfast there, too. Our culture arranges, rather proudly, to have an annual day when a child can come to work with a parent, to see the parental workplace—a far cry from life on a family farm. Parents were by all odds the moral arbiters for their children. Some modern parents seem to have abdicated that role entirely, and society seems to reinforce such abdication, by blaming the school system for not instilling better moral values. A cynic looking at our contemporary scene might say, of this fifth commandment, "Honor your father and mother? What's there to honor?"

Nevertheless, the instinct to honor is astonishingly strong. When social scientists ask young people to name their heroes, a majority still put a father or mother or both at the head of their list. We shake our heads in despair at the shortage of worthy role models in a society which seems to make so much of entertainers and professional athletes, but when the ballots are finally counted, it appears that young people are still rather old-fashioned: They think well of their mother and dad. The family instinct runs deep. It can withstand a shocking amount of abuse and broken trust.

The situation often changes, however, when the child becomes an adult. The person who seeks help from a psychiatrist is likely to conclude that his or her problems can be traced back to some parental failure. "I skip the first two words of the Lord's Prayer," a man tells his pastor, "because I'd hate to saddle God with the image of the father I know." "I'm setting out on the worst job of the year," a woman said. "I'm looking for a Mother's Day card that will be respectful without expressing some affections I can't imagine feeling." The attendants at any nursing home can identify several aged parents who are rarely, if ever, visited by their children, even though the adult children are only minutes away.

The fifth commandment is very realistic. It doesn't ask that a child have greeting card sentiments toward a parent, or that one love a parent; it insists rather, that we *honor* our parents. For some of us, that's easy, because our parents were basically kind and loving people. They may not have been perfect, but our memories of them are bathed in gratitude. But the commandment doesn't say, "Honor your parents if they deserve it," or "Honor your parents to the degree that they merit honor." The commandment provides no exceptions and no modifications, because the commandment isn't speaking of what the parent deserves. It is speaking of the child's own welfare, and of the larger welfare of society as a whole. As the apostle Paul pointed out many centuries later, "This is the first commandment with a promise: 'so that it may be well with you and you may live long on the earth' " (Ephesians 6:2-3).

The fairy tale I recounted earlier puts the matter at a poignantly personal level, and a true one: It's no fairy tale that children learn how to treat their parents by watching how their grandparents are treated. But the rules also operate at a broader, more philosophical level. It can fairly be said that our whole social structure is built on the foundation of the home. If children do not learn to honor their parents, they are given little basis for honoring anything or anybody: teachers, police officers, religious leaders, employers, government.

That's a frightening thought, isn't it? But that's the wisdom of the fifth commandment. Honor your father and your mother—not simply because such an idea appeals to you, and not necessarily because they deserve it; honor them for your own sake and for the sake of the future of your nation and of your children—"that your days may be long in the land that the LORD your God is giving you" (Exodus 20:12).

This commandment comes at an interesting place among

the ten. The ancient rabbis felt that the Commandments were divided on two tables so that one contained those laws having to do with our duty to God, and the other those laws having to do with our duty to humanity. This commandment is on the first tablet, as the last of the laws of piety toward God, because for children, parents stand in the place of God. So the Talmud said, "When a person conducts himself by honoring his mother and father, God is heard to say, 'It is as though I were living with them and they honored me.' " A thirteenth-century rabbi, probably Moses de Leon, put this relationship in very human yet very mystical light: Father and mother should be honored as God is honored, he said, because "all three have been partners in thy creation."

Needless to say, some parents make it very difficult for their children to see them in this way. And so does our culture. When popular culture pictures sex as a mating game, with emphasis on the pleasure of the moment, children are an incidental result. Under such circumstances, it's hard to think of ourselves as products of a partnership between woman, man, and God. The Psalmist said that it was God

> . . . who formed my inward parts;
>   you knit me together in my mother's womb. (Psalm 139:13)

But our culture calls that collection of mystery and potential a fetus. Somehow something is lost in translation between the language of the biblical poet and the language of the scientific laboratory.

So our generation has a poor foundation for a belief in honoring parents, because the ideas of conception and pregnancy are trivialized. If God was an instrument in my conception, and attended my development in the womb, my person is of such excellence that I will, of course, honor the humans who participated in the process. But the case is quite different if my whole prenatal biography can be cast in language which is exclusively naturalistic. Mind you, I am not denying the natural elements; but I am saying that they are not enough, that the story they give is lacking in plot, mystery, and excitement.

Our generation has another problem, too, in our ambivalent feelings about the past. In one sense, it fascinates us. A vast number of American small towns are now sustained by antique shops; it seems that everyone wants to purchase something which will give a tie to the past. Restaurants have cashed in on the same mood; no theme seems more popular than ersatz nostalgia. But beyond these quick acts of obeisance to the past, we see it only as something that is outdated. We have grown beyond its standards; its truths are more quaint than significant. And since to honor our father and mother is to pay respect to the culture they represent, we're content to settle for a washtub that can be converted into a magazine rack.

Strangely enough, Jesus seems to give us mixed signals about honoring parents. On the one hand, we think of the one biblical record of his childhood, his visit to the Temple as a boy of twelve. Somehow he became detached from his parents—which wasn't difficult, in a culture where children were safe in the larger community of their extended family—and ended up in the temple. There he became engaged in conversation with the learned teachers of the law, who were "amazed at his understanding and his answers" (Luke 2:47).

It must have been a heady hour for the boy Jesus. Because we know these stories so well, and because they are sacred stories, we often miss the human elements. But Luke is very clear, if only by implication, when he tells us that when they returned to Nazareth, Jesus "was obedient to them" (Luke 2:51). Luke realizes that Jesus might easily have asserted some independence from his parents after this experience of recognition and esteem, and he wants his readers to see how significant it is that Jesus goes back to being just a village boy who does his parents' bidding. He was, indeed, honoring his father and mother.

On the other hand, Jesus also said, "Whoever comes to me

and does not hate father and mother, wife and children, brothers and sisters, yes, and even life itself, cannot be my disciple" (Luke 14:26). Granted, the word "hate" had a different quality in a setting where a point was often made by hyperbole. Nevertheless, Jesus is clearly telling us that his will and his kingdom must matter more to us than even our most cherished human ties. He demonstrated the point on one occasion by identifying himself more with his followers than with his blood family, including even his mother (Mark 3:31-35).

Even so, Jesus is saying only what the Jewish scriptures had always taught—that God is the final arbiter in all of life's issues. It is the duty of parents to instruct children in the law of the Lord; they were not only to keep the laws themselves, but to "recite them to your children and talk about them when you are at home and when you are away" (Deuteronomy 6:7). The law is the end of the matter, not parents; and the value of parents is in their conveying of the law to their children. The issue, always, is keeping the faith. And if we are to keep it into the future, we must honor our parents, who are the tie between the past and the future.

Perhaps no factor in contemporary life is more alarming than the way parents have abdicated their teaching responsibility. It is popular to say, "Our hope is in the next generation," but of course it is patently untrue; our hope is in the past generation—or perhaps, more exactly, the one that is currently becoming past. The next generation is quite unlikely to come up with moral commitments better than those their forebears have taught them. If the future is to be what it ought to be—if it is to be wonderfully right—it will probably be because the current generation has laid a foundation of ethical character.

Professional scholars are not inclined to cry wolf, especially in matters of moral standards; their position is usually one of scholarly detachment. But Daniel Walker Howe, the Rhodes Professor of American History at Oxford University, insists that "American society needs to find some way to reassert the moral values on which the country was founded, to proclaim and defend them in family, church, and school, so as to inscribe them in individual personalities" ("America's Communitarian Roots," *Books and Culture,* November-December 1996, p. 24). Why? In order to get the "full realization of the potential of each individual."

That's what the fifth commandment promises. Honor your parents, honor your heritage, and your days will be long in the land; your future will be unlimited. The past is not a barrier which fences us in; it is a foundation on which we can build. Honoring the past and acknowledging its gifts makes us greater, not smaller. When someone belittles or demeans his parents, he diminishes himself. And when a person excuses her failures by reciting the errors of a parent, I think the right response might be, "Grow up! If you can perceive the mistakes of your parents so clearly, you must surely be perceptive enough to know how to remedy them."

Just now a new generation looks to its parents, and as I've said, it's frightening to see that so many in this generation of parents tend to abdicate the parental responsibility. We expect the schools to do our job, or some social agency, or perhaps some new law. And, of course, we can always quote an ancient mantra, probably the one Adam spoke to Eve after Cain went wrong: "Kids just don't listen, do they?"

As a matter of fact, kids *do* listen. That's how they come up with the standards they have. The failure is not in their listening but in our speaking. We must speak winsomely, convincingly, and with integrity, because we will have to be heard over a bewildering cacophony of competing voices. When Abraham told Isaac what to do, the only adverse counsel would come from an irresponsible servant or perhaps a passing trader. He didn't have to worry about disc jockeys, the Internet, rap musicians, or the corner newsstand. Yes, it is difficult for today's parent to be heard.

But the next generation is still listening. And the next

generation, like every generation before it, still gives greater weight to a parental statement than to any other kind.

Now consider this definition: "Parents" are not just blood or adoptive kin; every person who reaches adulthood gains some sort of parental influence over some younger person. Say what we will about the failure of the young to respect their elders, they still do. That's where they get their ideas and their standards, like it or not.

So embrace this good commandment, this lovely gift of heritage. Do you want to have a future? Then accept the blessing of the past. Would you like for tomorrow to radiate hope? Then ponder yesterday and the people who have made it—especially the people closest to you. They are not perfect, even as we are not perfect. But they are our foundation, and we must wisely build upon them.

Look at a house as you lay aside this book, any house—a condominium, an apartment, a suburban estate, a trailer park—and remind yourself that the future rests on that house, and millions of others like it. All of our institutions—education, law, government, world peace—rest ultimately upon this fine point of adult-child respect and integrity. Under God, the future of our race is quite unlimited. We will dwell long in the land if we honor our father and our mother.

CHAPTER 6

Part of the Mainland

....

EXODUS 20:13: You shall not murder.

You shall embrace life.

*I*f we had written the ten commandments, we probably would have begun with this one. After all, what is more sacred than life itself? Our profane world surely would not put "Thou shalt not take the name of the Lord in vain" ahead of this one; and as for "Remember the sabbath day"— well, that seems trivial and sectarian compared with something so basic as the taking of human life.

But our contemporary, quite secular culture has very little context for understanding the role of the sacred in human life, and therefore cannot really understand that we will never know how to deal with life—our own or our neighbor's—except as we begin with a right relationship with God. Indeed, unless God is our context, how do we begin to understand the sublime gift of life? History demonstrates that to the degree that we diminish God, the author of life, we also diminish life itself. This is not to say that the atheist or the agnostic does not believe in the importance of life; it is only to say that when God is incidental in the thoughts of society, life itself becomes incidental, because its sacredness is in question. Come to think of it, the atheist or the agnostic may be somewhat more sensitive to the God-issue than the thoroughgoing secularist, because God is at least an issue to those who take the time to deny or doubt God, while God hardly enters into the thoughts of the secular mind.

All of this is to say that the sixth commandment may be in greater peril in our time than in most periods of human history, and for that reason, it is more desperately needed.

Life has, indeed, become very cheap. This is not because my neighbor hates more fiercely than did the nineteenth-century neighbor, but because my neighbor has become more inured to death and, in fact, to murder. For instance, those who understand life in America's inner cities say that great numbers of young men (especially African American young men) don't expect to live into middle age; death is too constant a threat. The person who doesn't expect to live can hardly care much about my living—not because he or she is an especially bad person or innately violent, but simply because he or she has lost the natural awe of life. How can I hold your life in regard if the value of my own life is minimal? When I embrace life in myself, I am more likely to embrace it in you, and when I embrace life for you, my own life becomes not only more sacred, but also more grand and fulfilled.

I am reminded of the sublime wisdom and the exquisite beauty of that seventeenth-century poet-preacher, John Donne. During weeks of serious illness, as he lay in his rectory, he heard over and over the tolling of the funeral bells at his church. With each insistent tolling, he wondered who from his parish had died. Then at last he replied to himself, "Never send to know for whom the bell tolls; it tolls for thee."

Why? In what way is the death of any person my death? Because, as Donne wrote, "No man is an island, entire of itself." And he continued:

> Every man is a piece of the continent, a part of the main; if a clod be washed away by the sea, Europe is the less . . . any man's death diminishes me, because I am involved in mankind . . .

Unintentionally, Donne was writing a commentary on the sixth commandment. This brief, staccato statement, "You shall not murder," is intended not only to protect me from the loss of my life; it also protects me from the loss of my neighbor. When my neighbor dies, my life is made smaller. Both my neighbor and I are part of the mainland of life; if my neighbor dies, I am the less, and if I die, my neighbor is, to some degree, impoverished.

Who is my neighbor? My neighbor is all humanity—not just the person next door, or the person inherently dear to me, but all who have human blood in their veins. When Cole Porter, the popular twentieth-century lyricist, wrote, "I've got you under my skin," he was describing the intensity of one person's romantic love for another, particular person. But his words are religious, as well as romantic. Whether I love you, ignore you, or hate you; whether you are my dear friend, a nameless figure in a passing automobile, or a listing in the telephone directory, I've got you under my skin. If I kill you, I kill part of my very self. Any person's death diminishes me, because we are both part of the human race.

We aren't likely to believe that, however, unless we see something sacred in the origins of human life. Hitler could exterminate masses of humankind because he measured the worth of persons by the accident of geography and ethnic heritage rather than by the fact of divine origin. Twentieth-century totalitarian systems of both the left and the right have wiped out people with impunity because in those systems the state is more important than the individual.

What makes the individual so important? After all, we are creatures of the dust, and to the dust we return. Life is really quite cheap; ten thousand obituary columns make the point every day. War and famine stack up bodies like cordwood, and the highways take their toll not simply at the exit gates but in the grisly accumulation of accident fatalities. How can one think that life is sacred when the television dramas dispose of so many lives with such astonishing varieties of dispatch every evening? And in the television news which ends the day, we discover that what we have watched in fiction has been happening in fact even while we were sitting in our living room or den. How can anyone in such a world as ours dare to feel that life is sacred? Even our latest knowledge seems to be against it. After all, how can we still find mystery in life when we have the genetic code?

As a matter of fact, the mystery is now more wonderful than ever, and the answer is both more simple and more complex. Now that we know that the most subtle details of our person are written into our genetic code, we have a new basis for saying with the poet, "I am fearfully and wonderfully made" (Psalm 139:14). And it ought to be easier to continue,

> Wonderful are your works;
>   that I know very well.
>   My frame was not hidden from you,
>   when I was being made in secret,
>   intricately woven in the depths of the earth.
> Your eyes beheld my unformed substance.
> In your book were written
>   all the days that were formed for me,
>   when none of them as yet existed. (Psalm 139:14b-16)

The genetic code says scientifically what the Hebrew poet said with eloquent faith—that each of us is a wondrous creation. Not only is Einstein remarkable, or Mother Teresa, but so is the person we think of as utterly average—or less!

The creation story explains why. We are made in the image of God, the inspired writer said (Genesis 1:26-27). And still more specifically, the very breath of God is in us (Genesis 2:7). Fearfully and wonderfully made? That's hardly strong enough. Indeed, are there words which can describe the quality invested in us? If we are fearfully and wonderfully made, how ought we to treat one another? And how dare we take the life of another, when that life comes not simply by human union, but by the act of God in whose image we are made and whose breath we share?

I referred earlier to the bond of our human blood. But blood isn't our most profound bond. Our most profound bond is our *breath*. It is not simply our breath of life, significant as that is; our breath, as humans, is divine breath. It is what we have in common, across all ethnic and racial differences, far beyond all our intellectual, cultural, and economic differences. When I embrace my neighbor, I embrace my breath sister or brother; and if I kill or diminish another human creature, I violate the very breath of God.

Jesus showed us that the simple and direct understanding of this commandment is not enough.

> You have heard that it was said to those of ancient times, "You shall not murder"; and "whoever murders shall be liable to judgment." But I say to you that if you are angry with a brother or sister, you will be liable to judgment; and if you insult a brother or sister, you will be liable to the council; and if you say, "You fool," you will be liable to the hell of fire.
>
> (Matthew 5:21-22)

On the one hand, Jesus is insisting that we look at our hearts, our motives, and our thoughts. We conventionally civilized people wouldn't think of murder; not because our spirits are so refined, but because we are so conscious of the penalties involved. Besides, murder is messy business, and we are generally tidy folks. Most of us, in fact, wouldn't even hit another person, and certainly we wouldn't want to draw blood. But to be angry is quite another matter. It comes within the bounds of our cultural conduct, especially if we can use such a word as "indignant"; with that synonym, anger becomes sophisticated and almost essential. As for insulting, if it is done really well—that is, if it is the kind of putdown which Oscar Wilde might have crafted—we will not only do it, we will boast to others about having done it. And though "you fool" goes a bit far for civilized folk, we might indulge it under certain circumstances—say, with a telephone solicitor or an errant driver.

So now the question: Is there something of a killer in every one of us? Are we harboring violence just below the surface of our urbanity? Is there a meanness in us of which we ought to be ashamed, and for which we need forgiveness? These questions have to do with our hearts, our motives, our innermost thoughts.

On the other hand, there is the matter of the victim. Is the harsh word a close cousin to murder? Not in the obvious way, that our expostulation may lead to homicide; again, most of us are too "civilized" for that. But what about the pain we bring to the other person? Does this pain exhibit some elements of death?

Consider, for instance, two of America's presidents, Abraham Lincoln and Woodrow Wilson. We know that Lincoln was killed by an assassin's bullet, but what about Wilson? Herbert Hoover, who knew a good bit from his own experience about the pain of vilification, wrote a book entitled *The Ordeal of Woodrow Wilson*. Wilson was perhaps as idealistic a person as has ever served in the White House. He had a dream for world peace. Many national leaders disagreed with him, as they had every right to do. But some of the opponents became vile, hateful, and vindictive, as is frequently the case in the world of politics. They weren't satisfied to fight Wilson's ideas; they set out to destroy the man. They succeeded. He finished his term of office a completely shattered man. Perhaps Wilson was assassinated as surely as was Lincoln. It was a longer process, and more executioners pulled the trigger, but the result was the same.

Let's move out of history and the world of public personalities, and take some for-instances from scenes common to all our experiences. I think of a man who has raised a son to adulthood, dreaming that his boy will be a fine, noble human being. The boy, however, is selfish and thoughtless. He knows that his father is an honest, honorable man, yet he darkens his father's reputation by careless, unpaid debts. He gradually becomes known as a playboy, a shiftless ne'er-do-well who can't hold a job. One day the father dies. "Heart attack," the doctor says. "Murder," the sixth commandment replies. "A good father killed by a selfish, thoughtless, sinful son."

My words are harsh, because, of course, the boy wept at his father's funeral. But anyone who loves himself so much that he chooses his own way when he knows it is destroying someone else should never fool himself into thinking that he loves the other person. His actions prove too clearly that he is indifferent; and most indifference, when mixed with selfishness, comes out the same color as hate. And he who hates another is a murderer.

Or consider a girl who dreams of going to college so that she can become a teacher. But her parents and her neighborhood are poor—not only economically, but also in their perceptions and expectations. So they laugh at the girl. "*You* a teacher?" they say. "And maybe you'd like to be president of General Motors, too!" So they kill a girl's hope, and her future—and in doing so, they kill something of the girl herself.

It isn't necessary to perform physical violence in order to violate the sixth commandment. Surely that is part of what Jesus was saying. Nor is it necessary to curse and vilify someone; sometimes the most deadly form of hate is our failure to concern ourselves with another's need. Death is usually made up of a thousand pieces. That's why Jesus said it was murder to call a person a fool.

It is not enough to refrain from murder, or from cruel and hurtful language. I dare not be content with simply abstaining from the negative. I must embrace life, especially as I find it in you. And when I do, my own life is larger and greater.

When I think of the way kindness affects life, I'm sure I am living longer because of so many people who have embraced me. Have some people cursed me, or lied about me, or tried to diminish me? Of course! And they have cut into my life by doing so. But far more have by kindness enlarged, and yes, lengthened, my life. Frank and Mae Blackburn gave me a book when I was fifteen. They felt it would help me become a preacher. They not only blessed my life as a minister, they also set the sun shining about me. When I took their book from the shelf a few moments ago, I felt the glow of gladness in my cheeks. And I think of Mr. Bishop, who complimented me so frequently on my knowledge of the Bible as a teenager. Part of what I am and know today is because I tried to live up to what he expected of me. And there was Mrs. Witt, who treated my teenage insights as if they really amounted to something! What a gift that was!

This is just a minuscule sampling from an endless line of life-givers who have come my way. Of course, these people have made my life richer. But I'm just as sure that they have made it longer. I believe that life can be lengthened by words and deeds of kindness. If psychosomatic studies haven't already demonstrated as much, in time they will. But if length of life cannot be proved scientifically, let a word be said for other dimensions. Certainly such persons have made my life both deeper and fuller. These matters defy objective measurement, but all of us know when they happen.

So as surely as cruel and destructive words and manners deal death, words and deeds of kindness bring life. When a neighbor waves warmly as you pull out of your driveway, or a friend grasps your hand in a strong greeting or perhaps extends an affectionate hug, or when someone bothers to write a thoughtful note: In all such instances, you can feel the very flush of life and health.

This may be the most important argument in favor of a revival of old-fashioned manners. Courtesy takes time, whether it is a matter of letting another go first through a doorway or receive the table condiments before you do, but it is a gift of time which adds to the other person's worth. Some rules of etiquette may seem artificial or even pretentious, but in nearly every case they have their roots in thoughtfulness to others. A lifestyle which leaves no room for such gestures may occasionally save time, but only by taking life. It's a poor trade.

For a Christian, it isn't enough to say that we have never murdered anyone, or even that we rarely kill a small part of some other individual. We must fulfill what must surely have been the essence of this commandment, by blessing and enlarging life. In a world where so many quite casually damn, we ought very consciously to bless. We ought, that is, to make life longer, fuller, deeper, more exciting.

And when we do this for others, we will, of course, bring more life to ourselves. For inevitably I think better of myself when I think well of you—just as surely as I like myself less when I discredit you. One can't inflict death without in some measure dying. And happily, whenever we embrace life for another, we take a grander hold on our own lives—because we are all bound up together in this bundle of life. We are all part of God's wondrous mainland.

CHAPTER 7

Redeeming the Sacred

....

EXODUS 20:14: You shall not commit adultery.

You shall cherish the sacredness in you and your mate.

*A*t this point in history, the seventh commandment seems to be an endangered species. I'm not contending that adultery is committed more often in our day than it has ever been; that's a statistic that would be hard to prove. I am suggesting, however, that adultery is looked upon more casually or complacently today. Yes, it is still a subject for gossip, but its shock value is gone. When we hear of still another infidelity, we aren't quite ready to say, "Everybody's doing it," but we say something almost as telling: "Well, I guess that's the kind of world we're living in." That's a dangerous state of mind.

I suspect that you can judge the quality of a culture by that which shocks it. The naive are shocked by almost everything; we are shocked by almost nothing, and we're rather proud of it. The peril of leprosy, we're told, is not that it damages the extremities, but that it causes a loss of feeling in the skin. As a result, a patient may burn or injure himself or herself without knowing it, because the patient has lost the defense mechanism of pain. Similarly, adultery itself may not be as destructive to our culture as the virtual indifference with which we respond to it. By losing our capacity for ethical pain, we are weakening our moral defenses.

Someone striking a sophisticated pose might challenge the matter. What difference does it make, really, if a partner in a marriage seeks intimacy elsewhere? Suppose, in fact, both parties agree to an open marriage, where either or both can pursue other romantic interests; what harm is there? Those who see marriage as no more than a civil contract can reason that if the agreement isn't proving as beneficial as expected, a person can look elsewhere. If so, what harm is there?

Our answer to such questions will depend on our perception of marriage and our perception of ourselves. If we see marriage as involving wife, husband, and state, as is suggested by the marriage license, the issues may seem to be no more than pragmatic. But if we see marriage as a contract involving wife, husband, and God, the issues are very different.

The Old Testament law saw adultery as so grievous a sin as to deserve a death penalty (Deuteronomy 22:22-27). By such severe measures they meant to "purge the evil from Israel." That is, adultery was by no means a private matter, an act between "consenting adults"; it was an assault on the very community itself, and it must be dealt with for the community's sake.

It's interesting that Geoffrey Chaucer can be called in as a witness at this point. Chaucer treats moral matters rather playfully at times in his *Canterbury Tales,* but he sounds like both a legalist and a moralist when he talks about adultery. His parson argues that the commandment about adultery comes between those on murder and theft, because adultery is both the greatest theft and the greatest murder: It is a theft of body from the spouse, and a murder of the "one flesh" union of the spouses. Adultery was therefore no private matter; it was as much a public issue as theft and murder.

On the mystical side, Chaucer's parson contended that when a woman entered an adulterous relationship, she was not only stealing her body from her husband, she was also stealing her soul from Christ. The parson argued that this was worse than for someone to steal into a church and take the chalice, because the body is the temple of the Lord, and adultery is a taking of a vessel of grace.

Adultery, then, is a God issue. It is more than a code of sexual conduct, more even than a matter of morals. Perhaps it is not just coincidence that our synonym for adultery is *infidelity*, the word that is also a synonym for atheism. An infidel is someone who does not believe in God. Am I stretching the point when I suggest that the adulterer is also an infidel? Both the prophets of the Old Testament and the epistles in the New Testament pictured the relationship of God and his people as that of a marriage, and any violation of that relationship—especially to the Hebrew prophets—was an act of adultery. Surely nothing could be more clear: The Scriptures see sexual union as a holy act, with a quality so exquisite that the biblical writers consider it a fitting picture of our Lord's relationship with his people.

The Bible, you see, is not opposed to sex. As a matter of fact, it cares about it more than we do. The Bible might even indicate that the problem in our sex-saturated society is not that we think too much about sex, but that we think about it so poorly. Moses, Ezekiel, Hosea, Paul, and yes, Jesus, would probably shock us if they were to preach to our contemporary churches, because they wouldn't hesitate to discuss sexual conduct. And I think they would say, "Your culture talks about sex so much because it enjoys it so little. And it enjoys it so little because it understands it so superficially."

Our problem, especially, is that we forget what manner of persons we are. The Greek philosophers separated body and soul, seeing them as enemies. But the Scriptures look upon us as a unity: We do not simply have a body; we are a body. We do not simply have a soul, we are a soul. The body, then, is not an evil thing, but a part of God's good creation, woven through with soul.

Because the Bible has such an exalted view of the body, it cannot have a cheap or casual view of sex. This explains why the apostle Paul says so emphatically, "Shun fornication!" The issue is that our bodies are "a temple of the Holy Spirit," and that we are not our own (1 Corinthians 6:18-19). That puts the use of our bodies in a very different light. Contemporary culture says, "It's my body and I can do what I want with it," but Scripture says, "It is God's body, because the Holy Spirit dwells there."

Of course, that puts sexual union in a very different light—not only different, but higher, and with a much greater potential for joy and meaning. All of us know instinctively that this is true. We're told that sex is a basic appetite, like our need for food and water. But we sense that our sexual longing is something quite different from our need for food or sleep. Something spiritual abides in this relationship, something far more profound than a full stomach or a rested body. This sexual hunger is much more complicated than our hunger for even the best meal or the most desperately needed rest. Yes, there's a spiritual quality here. No wonder, then, that the biblical writers saw it as a vehicle for describing our relationship to God.

To explain this properly, the theologian must be a poet, and the poet must be a saint. Something in us is looking for an Eden; we are searching for something we have never really seen. As a pastor who has counseled with couples about to be married, I have heard literally hundreds of romantic stories. Each one has in it something of Adam awakening from his enforced sleep and exclaiming as he sees Eve, "This is it! This is what I've waited for!"

Every lyricist, novelist, or poet who tries to interpret romance and marriage simply does some variation on that Edenic theme. So a modern lyricist imagines "some enchanted evening . . . across a crowded room . . . and somehow you know . . . know even then . . ." It is only after Marjorie Morningstar is a nearly middle-aged matron that Wally Wronken realizes that there never really was a Marjorie Morningstar, and that he had created her ethereal loveliness out of his longings—his reach for Eden, if I may put words in the mouth of the novelist, Herman Wouk. Wordsworth said, in another generation,

> She was a Phantom of delight
> When first she gleamed upon my sight.

Nor does that glory have to fade. Anne Bradstreet, America's first published woman poet, must have known an exceedingly trying life in seventeenth-century New England. Yet she would write,

> If ever two were one, then surely we;
> If ever man were loved by wife, then thee;

and she felt in their love such a quality that she concluded,

> Then while we live in love let's so persevere
> That when we live no more we may live ever.

I don't think this earnest Puritan was trying to make a theological statement about marriage in heaven; she wanted only to say that the love they knew couldn't be fenced in by time and space. She felt they had caught a bit of Eden.

But where do we get such an unrealistic idea? It isn't from the marriages we've seen, perhaps not even from the best of them. Marriage is lived out in the crucible of ordinary, sometimes hectic days; it has to be fulfilled in the midst of budget-balancing, alarm clocks, conflicting schedules, and human weariness. Have the poets, novelists, and lyricists simply forsaken their sense? Where have they gotten their image of such perfection?

I don't believe they have lost their rational faculties. And I think I know where they've gotten their image, because their image goes farther back than cold logic can fully prove. You and I possess some tie to Eden that simply refuses to be destroyed. Something in us, Adam-like, keeps saying, "This is it! This is my missing rib! This is what I've waited for."

You and I have such an exalted view of marriage because we are what we are—creatures made in the image of God. We are never quite willing to be simply glands and gullets. We can't help being mystical. Sometimes this hunger for beauty gets us into great trouble. I'm sure that many infidelities begin with such a longing, when two persons who are disappointed in their present unions begin feeling that they have found their dream in someone else. That's why our longing needs to be understood. This quest for the exquisite which so often culminates in an affair ought to be turned instead into a more passionate drive for fulfillment in the union which already exists.

But the longing itself is a product of who we are. Deep down, we keep looking for Eden. The body looks for more than its body, because something in us knows that there's more to the body than flesh, blood, and sinews. We are, indeed, fearfully and wonderfully made, and that wonder is never greater than in our sexual longing, because at its best, that longing involves body, mind, and spirit. Instinctively it reaches for a perfection which may not be out of reach, but which calls for more than we are ready to give; and, of course, our contemporary culture, with its passion for instant gratification, makes us all the more impatient with the frustrations of our quest.

But if our culture has accentuated the problem, it didn't invent it. Effective marriages have always been difficult to achieve. A long-ago rabbi, Jose ben Halafta, said that since creation God has engaged in making matches, and that it is a task as difficult as dividing the Red Sea! We make it still more difficult for God by our style of cooperation—or lack thereof!

When I put together the findings of sociology and psychology, the insights of novelists and playwrights, and my own observations of the human race, I have concluded that adultery is rarely driven simply by lust. Yes, there are serial adulterers, but probably their conduct has no more to do with sex than does the conduct of the rapist; whereas the rapist is driven by anger, the serial adulterer is driven by ego and by the hunger for power. But the typical person, male or female, who gets involved in adultery is more often captured by longing. They're sure there's some magic out there, some experience of exquisite beauty, and that now they have found it. "This is no sordid affair," the man or woman comes to the pastor's study to tell me. "It's something so beautiful, something I've dreamed of all my life."

Of course! And that's what makes adultery so complicated. That's why, at the height (or depth) of such a relationship, the parties will forget their children, their sacred vows, their jobs, their future, and their God.

They will especially forget how they are complicating their lives and their psyches. The Talmud teaches that when a man who has been previously married marries a woman who has been previously married, four persons go to bed. We bring who we are into each human relationship, and the more intimate the relationship, the more complicated the bringing. Those who claim a certain kind of sophistication say that it's an advantage to be sexually experienced, but such experience clouds the psyche and confuses spiritual perception; and because we humans are spiritual creatures, the most important quality in our experiences is spiritual. Counselors often say that the most important sexual organ is the brain. Not quite. It's the soul.

That brings us back to our earlier question: What's so bad about adultery? In a sexually open society, with "mature," consenting adults, what's wrong with adultery? The pragmatic answer is that it doesn't work. Once again, the commandments of God are not arbitrary rules, not the picayunish strictures of a petty divinity; they are our best assurance of our finding the good life. Yes, adultery is wrong because it violates the law of God. But the law is made to fit the kind of persons we are. The worst thing about adultery is that it just doesn't work. It doesn't give us what we're looking for.

If we were purely physical creatures, adultery probably

wouldn't matter. The satisfaction we seek would be a matter of glands and appetites. But you and I are spiritual creatures. We want to mate, not because—animal-like—it is a certain time of the month. Nor is it simply because we are driven to reproduce, because the hunger continues to exist long after we have lost the ability to reproduce. Because we are spiritual creatures, we want to communicate, and we want to communicate at a level where vocabulary is inadequate and where words cannot carry the weight. Isn't it interesting that our best spiritual communication often comes through physical channels: when a baby's hand touches the face, a friend gives an embrace at the graveside, or a spouse reaches out in intimate caring. According to the creation story in Genesis, the breath of God is in our mortal frames, and therefore our physical acts convey the spirit. Unfortunately, this continues to be true when the spirit is poisoned. For as surely as we express love, loyalty, and compassion with a touch, we can express hate, anger, and resentment with the touches of violence. We are spiritual creatures for good and for ill—and if we choose not the good, we employ the ill. But one way or the other, we can't separate the physical and the spiritual, because we are spiritual creatures. In the language of Paul, our bodies are the temples of the Holy Spirit.

The consummate tragedy of our day is that we no longer know this. Our generation, more knowledgeable about sex than any generation in human history, may well know less about the fullness of sex than its predecessors. Perhaps the worst thing our easy-sex culture has done for us is to caricature sex, to make it one-dimensional. We rarely have a chance to explore the spiritual side of this most intimate human experience, because our culture doesn't really grasp that it exists. We grope after it in our romantic songs and our sentimental stories, but rarely reach it.

In most cases, we mistake the wrapping for the gift. It's the wrapping, after all, which is given all the play in our popular culture—the seductive body, the insistent persuasion, the intrigue of the forbidden. Perhaps we shouldn't be surprised that these are the elements that our culture emphasizes, because it is so much easier to show a well-turned thigh or a rippling pectoral than a lifelong loyalty. It's very hard for a camera to say, "For better, for worse, for richer, for poorer, in sickness and in health," because such words have to be lived out over months and years, and because such a concept is in the realm of the spirit, not in the measure of a photograph.

How good of God to equip us with bodies which are wonderfully spiritual, possessed of longings which are driven by both glands and soul! Fearfully and wonderfully made? Indeed! So having entrusted us with such powerful—indeed, combustible—equipment, God also left instructions for its use: "You shall not commit adultery." Or to put it another way, "You shall cherish the sacredness which is inherent in you, and in your mate"—because this is the only way it will work. That's the way you and I are made.

CHAPTER 8

To Each His Own

....

EXODUS 20:15: You shall not steal.

You shall become a larger person.

As long as our world has a population of two, we will need the eighth commandment. Every family, every pair of college roommates, proves as much when someone cries, "Who took my shampoo?" or "Who has my favorite pen?" We may say, altruistically, that material possessions aren't important—and they certainly aren't to be compared with human relationships, or with our relationship to God. But our possessions *do* matter, because they are extensions of ourselves. Property is sacred because it is the fruit of our labor and our intelligence, and often because it is tied to some of the deepest elements of memory and sentiment. If someone steals my property, he or she is stealing part of my very person—and with it, part of my human dignity and my chance to make of my life what I want it to be. Property is important, not necessarily because we are materialistic, but because property is so much a part of our very person, including memory, achievement, and dreams.

When I contemplate how comparatively simple life was in the world of ancient Israel, I think this commandment must have been written more for our age than for theirs. There were so few things to be stolen in that ancient, agrarian world, and so few ways to steal. Archaeologists reveal a very basic way of life when they find the remains of a village from the time of the patriarchs. It's mainly potsherds, weapons, and tools. There weren't many things to be stolen, beyond these few items: livestock, grain, and, of course, gold and silver. But the modern thief begins with automobiles, then appliances, computers, and household silver. And money, too—there's no prejudice against money—including that peculiar modern form of money known as the credit card.

Modern methods of stealing are even more impressive in their variety. In ancient Israel, theft was an outright thing; there was no need for such terms as petty larceny, grand larceny, fraud, embezzlement, and myriad variations thereof. Today a clever trader can steal from thousands of people at once by manipulating the market in a particular stock. That's a far cry from the biblical thief who managed to carry off a newborn lamb. A public official can take advantage of his office to gain various kinds of personal benefits. It's hard, in such cases, to trace the character of the theft and the specific victims, but the definition is the same. Then there's the small-time con artist who persuades the widow to have her furnace replaced when it is in perfectly good shape. And who could forget the persons—their name is legion—who steal from the government by way of their income tax statements? The eighth commandment can be put into four words in its ancient form, but if we want to recast it today, we'll need a book. A library, even! So we need this commandment, no doubt about it.

The complexity of our society complicates theft and its consequences. So many factors in our society make it easy to cheat. The small-town merchant of another generation knew that dishonest practices would soon put him out of business, but the marginal operator in urban settings can survive for generations; anonymity is a cloak for the unprincipled. In our culture, it can be hard to be honest with your employer in giving a full day's work if other employees choose to work at an indifferent pace. In some places, a really industrious worker is highly unpopular with his or her colleagues. The person who fills out an honest expense sheet may be told by coworkers that she is ruining it for everyone else. The employer who tries to treat workers fairly is at a disadvantage with competitors who are less ethical.

And how does one interpret honesty in dealing with corporations? I remember the university professor who raised the philosophical question in a graduate class: Is it possible to cheat a corporation? After all, a corporation isn't a person; how can you cheat a nonperson? How does one relate, for example, to the long distance telephone carrier? What's a $1.75 call to a company that counts its operation by the billions? Previous generations would have thought a long time before pilfering an item from the neighbor who ran the corner grocery store, but there's no such personal face on the huge corporate grocery chains. Community restraints are gone in an impersonal, corporate society.

So it is with the consequences of our conduct. When someone steals, we all pay for it. Because a suburbanite tucks a sweater into a shopping bag without paying, the store will cover the cost by increasing the price for all of its customers. Merchants estimate that the price of products is raised 2 to 5 percent in order to cover the cost of shoplifting and employee theft. When your neighbor collects on a phony automobile loss, the insurance company must increase its rates to cover the loss. When some citizen gets a generous settlement from the Internal Revenue Service, the government has to pick up the loss somewhere—and that's where you come in. When someone steals, everyone pays. More than ever, as John Donne so aptly put it, no one is an island, entire to the self; we are all part of the mainland of life, and each person's conduct affects a multitude of others.

From time to time, social reformers have argued that the surest way to cut crime is to put an end to poverty. Anyone who has even a modicum of conscience ought to work by any and all means to reduce human suffering, but it is naive to think that an end to poverty will bring an end to crime. Statistically, thefts were a much smaller problem during the Great Depression, when poverty was widespread, than in our present, more prosperous times. Today, theft is only sometimes the result of need. It is driven more often by greed and by lack of moral or ethical conscience.

Consider, for example, those persons on Wall Street or in the Stock Exchange who manipulate finances in a fashion that is at least unethical if not flagrantly illegal. Do they steal (yes, that's the right word) because they are hungry, or in poverty? Hardly! Or what about the executive who fudges on her income tax, or the community leader who uses his influence to kill a twenty-five-dollar traffic ticket—do they steal because their children need shoes? Obviously not. They steal because they find some strange satisfaction in beating the game. When a middle-class or upper-middle-class woman shoplifts, stealing items she can easily afford and which she probably doesn't even need, we say that she is ill, that she is a kleptomaniac. Most of the stealing which goes on in modern American society is an illness. Call it *sin,* the most irrational illness of all. Only a small percentage of the stealing in our culture comes from need. By far the largest portion has deeper roots, in the state of our soul and character.

That deficiency shows most dramatically in the subtlest form of theft, our stealing from life. Centuries ago, Basil put it with startling directness: "When someone steals a man's clothes, we call him a thief; shouldn't we give the same name to one who could clothe the naked and does not?" That is, what do we owe to life, and to our fellow human creatures? If I have enough (and what an elastic word "enough" is, when it comes to measuring our material resources!), don't I have some obligation to those who do not?

How dare I say that what I have is mine, when in truth I got it through so many others? I'm not speaking of inheritance; what my working-class parents were able to leave me in their will was, by contemporary measure, less than a month's pay. But they, and so many, many others, gave me so much more. How dare I vote against school taxes, unless they are manifestly unwise, when someone's taxes paid for my education long ago? How can I ignore an appeal from a college, when I remember that my tuition paid only a limited portion of the costs of my college education? And how can I go into a park, an art museum, a concert hall, or a church without feeling my debt to the people who gave to make these places possible?

I've come to realize that I have lived most of my life among the best of people—the givers. I've grown up in the church, an institution which, in America, is sustained entirely by voluntary giving. About the only other institution in which I have had continuing membership is service clubs. They, too, are giving organizations: Rotary, with its massive scholarship program and its more recent involvement in world health care; Kiwanis, with its high level of community involvement; and Lions, with their eyeglass program.

But sometimes I find myself talking with someone whose whole life revolves around their money, their golf club, and their vacation site in Florida, Arizona, the Riviera, or the mountains of North Carolina. They spell their life in Comfort, with a capital C, and they have not the slightest sense that they ought to share what they have. Under pressure, they offer a token gift to United Way or to their college fraternity, but the gift is in no way relevant to their resources. Well, I'd rather sit next to a career pickpocket, because I consider the pickpocket a more honorable person.

The prophet Malachi was nothing if not direct: "Will anyone rob God?" he asked (Malachi 3:8). His predecessor, the prophet Haggai, was not quite so succinct, but he was even more testy: "Is it right for you to live in expensive houses, while my temple is a pile of ruins?" (Haggai 1:5 CEV). Wealth is a crucial responsibility, and if we do not use it generously, we rob God and we rob life. It's important to observe that most of us are wealthier than we generally acknowledge. Our tastes and our expectations rise with our income, so that the person with three cars and a massive house may, with all earnestness, plead poverty—or at least, straitened circumstances. As the wise man said, the eyes of man are never full.

What all of this means is that stealing can be a passive act as well as an active one. The sin of commission is to *take* money that belongs to another. The sin of omission is to *keep* money that I ought to give to another.

The commandment against stealing obviously protects the structures of our social order, but it also protects the essence of who we are. Matthew Henry, the devout eighteenth-century preacher-scholar, who left us with the biblical commentary which bears his name, was once robbed while traveling through a dangerous area. Later that day, as he looked back on the experience, he wrote a series of reasons for giving thanks. One is especially significant to the eighth commandment. Henry gave thanks that he was the victim of the theft, and not the perpetrator. It is better by far to be the one stolen from than to be the one who steals. The one who is robbed loses only earthly goods. The thief loses so much more.

When we steal, we pay with a piece of our character, and that can never really be replaced. We also give up some measure of our self-respect. Perhaps we won't be apprehended for the theft, so the community will never know. But *we* will know, and we will think less of ourselves because of what we know. Somehow the opinion others have of us is never as significant as the respect we have for ourselves. Self-respect, once taken, is a dreadful loss.

An even greater loss is our right relationship with God. When we steal, we erect something of a barrier between ourselves and God. We do so anytime we break a commandment, and this one is no exception. When we put God at a distance, we are more susceptible to the numbing power of guilt. Guilt paralyzes us. We moderns sometimes think we know how to handle guilt, but we fool ourselves. Guilt has no real remedy short of a sense of rightness with God and with our fellow creatures. And guilt rarely stays the size of its original cause; it grows like kudzu.

Worst of all, when we steal, we weaken the conscience. This small voice, so strange and so insistent, is a great civilizing force. Without it, who can say what might happen to us? But it is relatively easy to muffle the voice of conscience. All we need to do is to commit a given sin several times. Before long, the once-insistent voice will all but disappear. When we steal— as with any other sin—we begin the process of muffling that voice. This is also true of the voice that tells us to give of our resources. We can argue with the voice of generosity until we convince ourselves that we have a right to all we own, and that it is inappropriate for anyone to suggest otherwise.

Stealing also does violence to our relationship to others. Obviously it can make us uneasy around others, because we're always afraid of being found out. The embezzler sometimes confesses relief when he or she is apprehended, because now he or she won't have to continue living under the dread of being discovered. Stealing is more than a crime against society; through guilt and fear, it also destroys social bonds. It does so, not only by our fear of being found out, but also by the suspicion with which we begin to view others. If I am a thief, perhaps my neighbor is, too. Once a person becomes a cheat, he or she has a nagging feeling that everyone else is also on the make. This is partly a matter of psychological self-defense; I find it easier to cope with my own shortcomings if I can convince myself that I'm no worse than anyone else. But it's no fun to live in a culture where we trust no one, and the thief condemns himself or herself to such a world.

Do you see what happens when we cheat or steal? We don't steal from the grocer, the government, or our classmates as much as we steal from ourselves. We rob ourselves of our self-respect, our character, and our sense of decency. We steal our own pure heart, and the best of our relationship with God. And if we slowly kill the voice of conscience, we have eliminated one of our best, truest friends. Such is the tragic irony of stealing; it is not only a sin but also a disastrous error in judgment, a fatal moral blindness.

The best things in life, the things which last and bless, are character, a clear conscience, self-respect, and a right relationship with God. We lose all of these when we steal. That makes stealing a pretty bad bargain.

The apostle Paul offered a better way. He wasn't talking about the eighth commandment, but his word applies. It's one of those Greek words which can't be translated into English, at least not without a paragraph. Our New Testament often calls it "kindness"; and while kindness is a magnificent quality, it is far short of the word that Paul used. *Chrestotes* was his word. The late William Barclay, the popular British Bible teacher, said that this was a word which meant to desire for others what one desires most for oneself.

That's quite the opposite of stealing, because when we steal we want what the other person has, rather than wanting them to have what we would want. It's also beyond our usual experience of giving. When we give, there is ordinarily no thought of duplicating our status, but simply of being helpful. And *chrestotes* is altogether different from the spirit of our age, the spirit which has been nurtured by the advertising philosophy that urges us to get something that our neighbor can't afford, or something that will set us apart from the common run.

What a better, exciting way *chrestotes* offers, with its wish for the best for our neighbor! Consider what you desire most, whether material things, accomplishments, recognition, or personal fulfillment—then imagine everyone being similarly blessed. Talk about a warm, fuzzy feeling! How large the heart feels when set in such a context of gladness!

I've seen this mood on a limited scale and have reveled in its beauty. The news media reported the story of a seventeen-year-old girl who gave a kidney to her mother to ensure her mother the life the girl wants for herself. In doing so, the young woman not only put herself through surgery and pain, but also reduced her own body's reserve, yet she looked jubilant on the television screen. Perhaps the most popular story of this kind in the closing decade of this century is that of Oseola McCarty, the Mississippi washerwoman who had to drop out of school in the sixth grade, but who celebrated her long life of faith, work, and stewardship by giving $150,000 to the University of Southern Mississippi for scholarships.

Hers is the spirit of *chrestotes*—wanting others to have what one wants most for oneself. She never got such an education, but she wanted others to have it. When word got out of what she had done, she said that people often asked her, "Miss McCarty, why didn't you spend that money on yourself?" Her answer, with a smile: "Thanks to the good Lord, I *am* spending it on myself" (*Guideposts,* September 1996, p. 5).

That is the point of the eighth commandment. The person who chooses not to steal—using the broadest and most demanding definition of that word—may suffer some temporary loss, but he or she becomes rich. When we take from others, we make ourselves smaller; we diminish not only the person whom we cheat or from whom we steal, but we also diminish ourselves. And when we turn life into a giving enterprise, we grow larger.

"You shall not steal." In other words, you shall become a larger person.

CHAPTER 9

Blessed Communicators

EXODUS 20:16: You shall not bear false witness against your neighbor.

You shall bless and be blessed by the truth.

*P*robably the greatest power given to us human beings is the power of the human mind. Its power is so vast, so pervasive, and so diverse that no one can imagine its potential.

The second greatest power is communication. Although communication depends on the mind for its resources, in a strange way it holds power over the mind. You see, what the mind unearths is useless until it is communicated, and the only way our minds can share their resources—whether noble or base—is by the process of communication.

It's no wonder, then, that one of the key phrases of our times is an explanation for all that goes wrong: "a breakdown in communication." Most cliches become absurd with continued use, but this one has survived because it is demonstrably true.

The ninth commandment protects not only the integrity but also the very worth of the power of communication. Powerful as communication is, it can be warped and distorted by any fool or scoundrel. The power to communicate, like the power to procreate, is distributed indiscriminately. We don't have to pass any test of mind or character in order to become a communicator.

So the ninth commandment declares, "You shall not bear false witness against your neighbor." This commandment applies especially to the court of law, where truth is a matter of life and death. But the Jewish people understood that it was meant to apply to the whole realm of human relationships, covering all forms of slander, defamation, and misrepresentation. Further, it applied to groups, races, and faiths, as well as to individuals. So while the Contemporary English Version may seem to oversimplify in its desire to be easily understood, it is nevertheless on target when it translates this commandment, "You shall not tell lies about others."

This translation makes sense, because in truth all the world is a courtroom. Everywhere and always, reputations are on trial. It is not only before judge and jury that you and I are called innocent or guilty; would that it were so! Such decisions are constantly being made at business luncheons, during telephone gossip, at parties, during coffee breaks, in letters, and in E-mail.

If truth is important in courts of law—so important that it is spoken under oath—it is even more important, and more in peril, in the courtroom of daily life. When people stand before a judge, they realize the solemnity of what they say, but in social occasions there is not only no oath, there also is an informality and a conviviality that can encourage easy, thoughtless speech. In the formal courtroom, the person on trial has a chance to hear the charges that are made against him or her. But in daily life, we rarely know what stories are being told or what judgments passed, and rarely do we have a chance to set the record straight.

All the world is indeed a courtroom. Unfortunately, rules of justice and human dignity have little chance in the complex, unrestrained court of daily life. The only protection for reputation and personal security is in the kind of human integrity which the ninth commandment calls forth: You shall not bear false witness against your neighbor.

It may well be that no sin is so universally popular as the sin of false witness, the sin of slander, the defaming of other persons. This is partly because all of us have the weapon, and because the weapon is so immediately available. We may not have a knife with which to cut someone, and we may not be strong enough to swing a bludgeon, but the tongue is always at hand, and we can use it with even our dying breath. Then, too, this sin can seem so innocent when compared with others. Many of us would never think of striking another person physically, but our sensibilities are not offended by repeating an unverified story. Some who would faint at the sight of blood are not at all disturbed by the sight of a battered reputation.

I am embarrassed to realize how often I have welcomed a destructive word about someone else. I haven't always pressed the messenger to confirm the truth of what was being said. Sometimes I have been secretly glad to hear the destructive word. And sometimes I have even passed on the unverified report. My conscience is sensitive enough that I have usually said, "This report may not be true," but such a disclaimer is easily lost in the transmission of salacious information. I need the ninth commandment.

False witness comes in many forms. The Old Testament itself indicates some possibilities in the different Hebrew words used in the two versions of the ten commandments given in Exodus and Deuteronomy. Exodus uses a word which means *lying* or *untrue.* In Deuteronomy, the Hebrew word means *insincere, empty, frivolous.* That's significant, because sometimes our false witness is not an outright lie; it is simply a frivolous, thoughtless word. We've heard a story about someone. We aren't sure of the facts, and we don't mean any real malice. Nevertheless, though we're not malicious and though our style is frivolous, we can do great harm.

One of my seminary professors, the late Ronald Sleeth, used to warn us against what he called "the libel of labels." Label someone, he said, and you may have done a libelous act. Call someone a radical or a right-winger, an extremist, a liberal, or a fundamentalist, and you have removed that person from serious consideration. Their ideas are discounted and their insights tainted because they've been labeled. I'm sure this problem has always existed, but it is worse in our time because our style of living encourages snap decisions. If we are the sound-bite generation—to use another label which may be libelous—we are especially susceptible to such quick and easy judgments.

One of the most subtle forms of false witness is inappropriate silence. Clovis Chappell, one of the most popular preachers from the middle third of this century, said that the person who listens to gossip is like the person who serves as a "fence" for the underworld thief. The thief would be forced out of business if there weren't someone to "fence" or handle his or her product. Just so, there could be no false witness if there were no listeners. The Jewish law condemned the person who gave false evidence as well as the one who, having evidence to the contrary, refused to give it. If we sit in silence while a reputation is being discredited, when we know the truth or have good reason to question what is being said, we become party to slander and to the destruction of that person. Silence is not always golden; sometimes it is criminal.

A close kin of silence, on the nastier side of the family, is the person who doesn't slander but simply raises questions. Someone says of a person, "She's a kind, loving human being," and the questioner answers, "Could be. But I'd know the truth if I lived with her for a week." There! That changes the score! This practice comes right out of the encounter between Eve and the serpent. The serpent didn't at first lie about God; he simply raised a question: "Did God tell you not to eat fruit from any tree in the garden?" (Genesis 3:1 CEV). So the seed of doubt was planted. We've been doing it ever since.

Slander is never worse than when we set out purposely to hurt or destroy another person. Sometimes it's a matter of revenge; someone has hurt us, and we intend to pay them back. More often slander is a product of jealousy; we resent another person's success, and we want to cut them down to size. That's a telling motive, of course, because it is a tacit admission that the other person is bigger—or at least, perceived to be bigger—than we are, so we want to reduce them to a level we can cope with. I wonder how often persons bear false witness against others simply because they are unhappy with themselves? All of us have known someone who is an equal-opportunity belittler; they really don't care who their target is, as long as they can diminish someone else. If there's any malice involved, it isn't really personal; it's simply malice against the human race. More particularly, it is the disguised cry of someone who is very unhappy with self. And so society— or whatever individuals come their way—pay a price for their unhappiness.

Almost surely someone is saying, "But what harm is done? What's a little malice now and then?" An old story puts it in painfully humorous terms. A Quaker had tried unsuccessfully to train his dog, Tray. At last he said to the dog, "I am a gentle man, so I will not beat thee. But I will give thee a bad name." So he turned Tray out into the street, calling him a mad dog, and before long someone killed him.

I've seen the parable become a reality. When I was a young pastor, I was privileged to have in my congregation a dedicated public official. He was working doggedly at a difficult job. For some reason the local newspaper began to attack him, and then he began receiving hate mail. He wasn't the kind of man who could endure lies and unfair accusations. One day he took a gun and killed himself. Slander did it. One feels utterly helpless and frustrated in responding to false witness. No matter how hard you try, you know you can't answer all the lies, nor can you correct all the misconceptions.

Worse yet, the residue of false witness seems to last forever—or at least, to outlive its victims. I was once maligned for a matter in which I had no guilt, and in time my integrity was well demonstrated. But a dozen years later, when a personal crisis put me in a vulnerable situation, I discovered that several persons were resurrecting the lie I thought was long dead.

I wonder if Shakespeare was a victim of malicious lies, or was he simply an astute observer of the human scene? At any rate, no one has ever put it better than he did in *Othello:*

Who steals my purse steals trash; 'tis something, nothing;

. . . .

But he that filches from me my good name
Robs me of that which not enriches him,
And makes me poor indeed. (act 3, scene 3)

In truth, slander is one of the most tragic of our human practices, because its influence is so far-reaching. Ultimately, our human relationships depend on trust. When people choose to deceive, all other laws become ineffective. Paul Johnson, the English historian and essayist, insists that ours is a universe of laws, including moral laws. If humankind ignores these laws, Johnson says, it is "at the risk of its social health and even its existence" (*The Quest for God*, 69). This is true at all levels of life. Peace between nations can be shattered by false witness as surely as can the relationship between husband and wife, parent and child, friend and neighbor.

Have you sometimes wondered, when a friend has spoken to you destructively of a mutual friend, if perhaps the telltale friend treats you the same way in your absence? We want so much to have someone we can trust. Whether in business, in friendship, or in romance, we want to feel we can count on the next person. Loneliness is probably the most poignant human pain, and the sting of loneliness is the feeling that there's no one we can count on. Diogenes went out with his lantern to find an honest man. Was Diogenes concerned solely for the public welfare, or was his search perhaps more personal? Was he hoping to find someone he could count on, someone who deserved the title of friend?

So the ninth commandment is not a restriction on life, social intercourse, and imagination; rather, it gives a foundation for all that is best in human communication. What good is it for me to cast delightful epigrams and scintillating figures of speech if you can't depend on what I say? If I speak with the tongues of men and of angels but taint my speech with malice and misinformation, I am worse than a sounding brass; I am a social Lorelei who will shipwreck lives. Some of my preaching students think I'm a crank about grammar, and they may well be right. But I wish all teachers would begin instruction by the ultimate rule of communication: Speak the truth. Human communication depends upon it. More than on agreement between subject and verb, more than remembering when to use the objective case.

But what about those instances when the truth itself is as deadly as slander? Gossip is not always lies or exaggeration; much of it is hard fact. Does the ninth commandment require us to ignore what is unpleasant or evil?

Certainly not. But love and good sense and Christian charity should make us think twice before we speak. I take a cue from King David. He was catapulted to the throne by a tragedy, the death of King Saul and Prince Jonathan in a disastrous defeat by their ancient enemies, the Philistines. Saul died in shame. Earlier, Saul had sought repeatedly to destroy David, but now David refused to find pleasure in Saul's downfall. "Tell it not in Gath," he cried, "proclaim it not in the streets of Ashkelon" (2 Samuel 1:20). There was no denying the facts, but there was no good in broadcasting them.

This is where conversation so often turns truth into gossip. It may be true that friends are getting a divorce or that a neighbor is being incarcerated for drugs, and it may be proper to pass this news to a mutual friend. Indeed, doing so may inspire prayer. But I am quite astonished at how quickly the sharing of such news degenerates into speculation and marginal malice. Some things, whether true or not, simply ought not to be talked about, because of the harm they will do.

The apostle Paul recommends a wonderful alternative, the way of love. "Love doesn't keep a record of wrongs that others do" (1 Corinthians 13:5*b* CEV). What a powerful restraint on slanderous communication! So often we pass along bad news ("Believe me, it's true. I wouldn't tell it if it weren't.") because we're settling an old score, and we're delighted that we can do so. And the apostle continues, "Love rejoices in the truth, but not in evil" (1 Corinthians 13:6 CEV). Some "hard facts" are also evil, and we should have nothing more to do with such matters than is absolutely necessary.

One more word from the apostle Paul. If we want to find the balance between truth and love, and how to keep the communication of fact from degenerating into gossip, the secret begins in the state of our minds. That's where Philippians 4:8 is so helpful:

> Finally, beloved, whatever is true, whatever is honorable, whatever is just, whatever is pure, whatever is pleasing, whatever is commendable, if there is any excellence and if there is anything worthy of praise, think about these things.
>
> (Philippians 4:8)

I was visiting with an old friend recently. We've had hundreds of lunchtime conversations over the past nearly twenty-five years, so we're pretty candid with each other. He is scrupulously honest; in the course of so many years, we've had occasion to discuss unpleasant news about persons and institutions. But I've never known him to revel in the muck. He can handle hard facts without malice. And I know why; he is a thoroughly positive person, who chooses to focus his mind on what is good, right, and hopeful.

What a power the Creator has invested in us in our ability to communicate with one another! And how marvelously we have come to refine and sharpen our powers of communication as we have added to our human vocabulary, so that we have words for almost every insight and experience. How dreadful, then, to destroy the very foundation of communication by untruth!

Our civilization stands or falls on the issue of truth. The

public demagogue destroys the political structure by casual lies, and the gossip destroys individuals by private lies. But those who love the truth lift communication to its highest levels. They bring a kind of transparent goodness to human relationships. Political discourse gains a quality of nobility, business negotiations enter a new realm of trust, and loneliness is driven into retreat, because we find those of whom we can say, "I can count on them."

Thus, those who hear the truth are blessed, because they know they invest their trust well. And those who speak it are blessed, because they have the joy of the pure in heart.

CHAPTER 10

A Matter of Vision

....

EXODUS 20:17 RSV: You shall not covet your neighbor's house; you shall not covet your neighbor's wife, or his manservant, or his maidservant, or his ox, or his ass, or anything that is your neighbor's.

You shall rejoice in your neighbor's having.

The first and the tenth commandments form bookends to this great body of law. They both deal with the intangible—the first, our relationship with the Almighty, and the tenth, our relationship with our own souls. Both involve matters which are nearly impossible for any law to define. After all, who can say when we are putting some other god ahead of the Lord God? And who can judge the boundary between proper, wholesome desire and covetousness? These are the most spiritual of the commandments. A graven image is an object, blasphemy is identifiable words, the sabbath is a given day, parents are real people—and, of course, murder, adultery, theft, and even lies are matters which can be identified. But coveting is a spiritual matter (negative, of course), as is failing to hold God first.

Because these two commandments are so spiritual, so intangible, they are quite beyond the ability of the law to enforce. Someone can say that you have bowed before a graven image, but who can say that you prefer another god, unless you announce it? The law can judge when we murder or steal, but who could dare to prove that I have coveted?

Who, that is, but God. And our own souls. Our own souls

will collect their dues on covetousness, as well as on our relationship with God. Coveting is a secret sin, sometimes so secret that we seem to hide it even from our own consciousness. But it will be revealed. Our souls will reveal it. Someone has said that covetousness is "the sin of sins" because it opens the door to so many other sins. If we covet our neighbor's spouse, we are in danger of slipping into adultery. If we covet our neighbor's possessions, we may easily violate the eighth commandment, theft—and perhaps also the ninth commandment, false witness, and perhaps even the sixth commandment, murder. Coveting enhances the power of other sins.

The dictionary defines "covet" as "to desire inordinately or without due regard for the rights of others." Let's understand from the outset that this is something different from desire. Of itself, desire is a good thing. Desire takes us from ignorance to knowledge, from poverty to abundance, from sickness to health. Without desire, the world would die of simple inertia. But desire becomes an evil power when the desire is for that which is wrong, or when the desire violates the rights of others. When my desire for even a good thing makes me covet what you have, my desire becomes a destructive force.

Some of the ancient Eastern religions seek a goal of nondesire. Perfect peace, they teach, is in wanting nothing. Buddhism teaches that desire is the cause of all suffering, so it seeks to put an end to desire. The Bible takes a very different position. It teaches that God has provided us with a universe full of good things, and that God intended us to enjoy and to benefit from these favors. As a result, we are constantly required to make decisions. It would be easier to rule out all desires than to regulate them. The handling of desire is a lifetime moral education.

Of course, the peril of coveting is built into desire, but to covet something is not simply to want *it* but to want what belongs to another. Thus it has to do with our feeling toward our neighbor. We want what the neighbor has—perhaps precisely because he or she has it. Their very having seems to awaken our desire. Apparently there is some psychological attractiveness in my neighbor's possessing. "Thy neighbor's" is clearly the operative phrase in this commandment, so that it is repeated with each example. It is not wrong to want a spouse, an ox, or an ass—or a car or a computer or a Super Bowl ticket—but it is quite another matter to want these things when they belong to my neighbor.

Covetousness is, no doubt, as old as the human soul. Obviously, it was an issue thousands of years ago in the agrarian economy to which the commandments were first given. But it is a particular peril in our time, partly because possessions form the most important symbol of attainment in our society. We have no titles or hereditary privileges, so we make "titles" for ourselves with house, boat, or car. Covetousness is also a particular peril for us partly because possessions are, in one measure or another, within the reach of almost everyone in the Western world. Coveting is a useless enterprise in many parts of the world, because most material possessions are unattainable. But in the West, coveting is endorsed by rational hope, because here a person may well get what his neighbor has—and more, too.

Isn't it ironic that the very fact of abundance has given new power to covetousness? One would assume that we might stop coveting once we're able to have so much, but it doesn't usually work out that way. Some years ago the late Walter Reuther, who was a key labor leader, contended that much strife in America would end when our economy reached a point where every family had two Cadillacs. But it just isn't so, because covetousness is not cured by getting. It has nothing— or virtually nothing—to do with what we have, or with what we need.

You see, covetousness is a state of mind, not a state of the economy. As long as our hearts are covetous, we will want what the other person has, no matter how much we have or how little he or she has. What's more, covetousness is not limited to material things, though obviously this is the main thrust of the commandment. We may envy our neighbor's popularity or position in the community. We may covet our neighbor's club membership, or we may even covet the office he or she holds in the church. Some of us are relatively indifferent to money and property but quite susceptible to other attractions; though we would not covet our neighbor's house or wardrobe, we might covet his or her social poise or reputation as a host or hostess. Coveting has many faces, and just when we think we are victorious over the last attractive face, a new one appears.

So how do we win the struggle with covetousness? Since desire itself is an essential in life, so that we must maintain a constant relationship with desire, how do we protect ourselves against that level of desire we call covetousness, the desire that destroys?

It's all a matter of vision. I have come to believe that covetousness is a sin which springs from poor vision—not physical vision, of course, but poor spiritual vision. There's some irony in this, since coveting often begins with the physical act of seeing: "I saw, I desired, I took" is the ancient formula (as old as Eden, come to think of it). When we covet, however, the worst irony is that we don't see enough.

For example, consider the thing itself. What is the value of the thing I covet? If I covet my neighbor's spouse, is that spouse of such value that I would trade my family, my sense of responsibility, my self-respect in order to gain that spouse? Or if I covet my neighbor's house, do I see its price? That is, do I ponder the payments my neighbor has to make, the strain of the mortgage, the burden of the upkeep? Or if I covet my neighbor's position of prominence—his or her place in the eyes of the public—do I see how tiresome it may be to live in a fishbowl of public attention?

Covetousness is almost always nearsighted. It sees the neighbor's destination, but it doesn't fairly estimate the length of the road leading there. After a classical pianist had completed a concert, an enthusiastic amateur said to the performer, "I'd give ten years of my life to play like that!" The pianist answered, "It cost me twenty." Most of the things we covet—at least, those that are worth having—are available if we're willing to pay the price of time and hard work.

But covetousness always looks for a shortcut. Perhaps that's why covetousness is riding high in our day. The very nature of our sped-up world has geared us to instant gratification. We want what we want immediately, if not sooner. So while we can see the good things our neighbor has, ranging all the way from success in work to a happy marriage, we can't see the length of the journey or the heat of the day which those attainments cost. We want to get our fortune with a lottery ticket, solve our personality problems in a weekend seminar, and get peace of mind with a packet of pills. It's the very nature of covetousness to be shortsighted, to look for instant pleasure.

The poor vision of covetousness is especially disastrous in what it does to our own person. Covetousness prevents our seeing what we have, or at least, of recognizing its value. Russell Conwell made famous the story of a wealthy Persian who heard that somewhere in the world there was a vast store of diamonds. He went to bed that night a poor man—poor, Conwell said, because he was discontented, and discontented because he saw himself as poor. He sold his farm and began a worldwide search for the acres of diamonds, until he had spent his entire fortune in the quest. After his death, they found in his old farm the acres of diamonds he had so feverishly sought, the famed diamond mine of Golconda. Conwell reminded his many audiences that each of us has "acres of diamonds" in his or her own backyard. He proved it in his own life by building the struggling Temple Baptist Church in Philadelphia into one of the great churches of its day, and with it, founding Temple University and the Temple Hospital.

The tragic figure in Conwell's speech reminds us to look again at what we have. Coveting always sees life's acres of diamonds somewhere else—in our neighbor's house or spouse or fame. And with all of our coveting, we grow dull to what we have. Shakespeare said it perfectly:

> Desiring this man's art, and that man's scope,
> With what I most enjoy contented least. (Sonnet 29)

This is the bitter irony of covetousness: It makes us blind to our own wealth, prevents our enjoying the beauty which is already ours. So many people don't enjoy the home they have because their eyes are captured by their neighbor's home; they don't truly drink of the friendships available to them because they envy those who live in the world of glamorous, sophisticated people; they don't drink in the color and quality of their own street because they covet a street in New York or Paris or London. Perhaps coveting does nothing worse to us than rob us of what we already have—including sound judgment about life's priorities.

Coveting, in fact, distorts our whole sense of values. Jesus said, "But strive first for the kingdom of God and his righteousness, and all these things will be given to you as well" (Matthew 6:33). As I said earlier, the Christian faith doesn't despise the things of this world; to the contrary, it considers them God's good gifts, intended for our pleasure and benefit. But it warns that we should keep them in their place—and that's *second* place. When we covet, we think some object or person or position will bring us happiness. That's far too great a burden to put on any person or thing. Only God can fill the God-shaped void. Having allowed God to fill the ultimate place in our lives, we can accept money, lands, clothing, honors, and people for what they are: worthy secondary factors in life. God must be kept at center.

Covetousness not only puts God in second place, it also dims our vision of God. I find that I am not inclined to envy anyone when my heart trusts God. It isn't that I have everything I shall ever want, or that I am completely content with my circumstances at any given time. But when my faith is right—that is, when I am seeing God rightly, for faith is nothing other than right vision—I have a deep confidence that whatever is best for me will come my way in proper time. If something is worth having, and if I am willing to apply myself to its proper pursuit, God will help me achieve it. If God does not bring it, I can rest peacefully in the knowledge that I'm better off without it.

But when my faith isn't right, when I'm not seeing God rightly, I remain focused on my desire—or, more accurately, on my neighbor's possession. As I said earlier, the key word in this commandment is *my neighbor,* so it's here that we need especially to examine our souls. So frequently we want something, not because we truly want it, but because our neighbor has it. Isn't it astonishing how the ordinary becomes extraordinary if our neighbor has one? The problem, of course, is that we see our neighbor as our *competitor* more than as our neighbor. Love, by Paul's definition, "is not envious" (1 Corinthians 13:4). Paul also said that we should "rejoice with those who rejoice, weep with those who weep" (Romans 12:15). Most of us realize that it is easier to weep with our neighbors than to rejoice with them.

Perhaps there is no more significant measure of friendship—and of Christian love—than our readiness to rejoice in our neighbor's gain, particularly when that gain is of a kind that appeals to us. A high school classmate reminded me at our fiftieth class reunion that I had won an award she had sought when we were juniors. For the life of me, I couldn't remember the competition, but I might have if I had lost. Our naturally competitive natures are like that.

So how much do we love our neighbor? Enough to rejoice in his or her good fortune? Covetousness, perhaps more than any other sin, invades my relationship with my neighbor. Isn't that ironic! It is my neighbor, the person close to me either geographically or emotionally, who is most likely to be my stumbling block on the tenth commandment. If only I could fulfill the second half of the great commandment and love my neighbor as myself, I might never again have to worry about the tenth commandment. After all, if I loved my neighbor as I love myself, I would find joy and fulfillment in my neighbor's gain. My neighbor's winning would mean as much to me, by definition, as would my own winning.

If that were so, how much bigger my life would be! If I define my neighbor as Jesus did in the story of the Good Samaritan, my neighbor is anyone with whom I come in contact. Suddenly I have reason to be grateful no matter where I look. Whoever in my circle of knowing enjoys some prosperity, some gladness of life, is automatically my benefactor because of the joy his or her gain brings to me. Under such circumstances, this world would hold more rejoicing than I might easily contain!

Such is the blessing of this tenth commandment. When I rejoice in my neighbor's having, I become wonderfully, almost unimaginably rich. When I covet, my life is so small and petty, but when I rejoice with my neighbor, my life has no boundaries. I feel better about myself, because I'm so much more likable when I'm not envious. I feel better about God, because I'm seeing more of God's goodness when I get out of my own small world. I feel better about life, because I see its blessings more clearly; I see what I have, instead of what I haven't.

All of this leads to a spirit of contentment. As more than one wise soul has observed, the richest persons are not those who have the most, but those who are happiest with what they have. Before the apostle warned that the love of money is a root of all kinds of evil, he put the matter positively: "Of course, there is great gain in godliness combined with contentment" (1 Timothy 6:6). Contentment is utterly incompatible with covetousness. To covet is to be discontent. To be content is to be in right relationship with God, with life, with one's own soul, and with one's neighbor.

Tauler of Strasbourg is remembered as a great fourteenth-century saint and mystic. One day he learned a lesson from an anonymous beggar. "God give you a good day, my friend," Tauler said as he met the beggar. "I thank God I never had a bad day," the beggar quickly answered. Tauler was silent for a moment, then said, "God give you a happy life, my friend." And the beggar answered, "I thank God I am never unhappy."

Now Tauler was nonplussed. "Never unhappy," he said. "What do you mean?" "Well," the beggar replied, "when it is fine, I thank God; when it rains, I thank God; when I have plenty, I thank God; when I am hungry, I thank God; and since God's will is my will, and whatever pleases Him pleases me, why should I say that I am unhappy when I am not?"

Tauler was now in awe of his new friend. "Who are you?" he asked. "I am a king," said the beggar. "A king!" said Tauler, half ready to believe it. "Where is your kingdom?" The man in rags spoke calmly, strongly. "In my heart," he whispered. "In my heart."

The tenth commandment leads the way to such a kingdom, and it is a large empire, indeed.

A Privileged People

*H*ow is it that the Israelites were willing to accept such a document as the ten commandments? After all, these commandments appear to be restrictions on life. At the very least, they're telling us what we ought to do, and something in us doesn't like to be told what to do. Even the word "ought" is offensive to us. What is it that could have made a body of laws so attractive to people that they would promise to be bound by them? Granted that saints, the kind of far-seeing souls who gave us literature like Psalm 119, might see the law as a blessing. But what of ordinary folk? How is it that they could be persuaded to accept a way of life that was clearly intended to fence them in?

The answer is given before the question is asked. The ten commandments are introduced by the statement, "I am the LORD your God, who brought you out of the land of Egypt, out of the house of slavery" (Exodus 20:2; Deuteronomy 5:6). Israel had a history. For more than four hundred years, it had been a nation of slaves. Then, without any action on their part to merit it, the people had experienced a series of miracles, culminating in their passage through the Red Sea and the subsequent destruction of the enemies who were in pursuit of them. It was on the basis of this experience that God had a right to give them a body of commandments. As the One who had given the people their freedom, God was now instructing them how they could make the most of that freedom.

That is, the commandments weren't born in a vacuum. They were the product of a relationship, and a gracious one, at that. If a stranger—even a divine one!—had given Israel these commandments, they would have been an imposition. "Who are you," Israel could justifiably have said, "to tell us how to live?" But their benefactor had a prior claim. When a university gave me a scholarship for graduate study, they included some stipulations for its use. That was their right, since they had made me their beneficiary. Just so, the One who gave life to Israel also gave them instructions for preserving the life they had been given. God now had a vested interest in this people, and with it a right, indeed an obligation, to see that the interest was not squandered.

Unfortunately, we seem to find it hard to remember the favors that have been done for us. The ironic comment, "How soon they forget," fits most of us at one time or another. We don't mean to be ungrateful, but our memories are short. And memory can be especially faulty when it is asked to bring up pictures one would rather forget. I find that people who come from a background of poverty have two ways of handling their past. Some deny it, or try to do so. Others gladly lay claim to it. Moses, and the great prophets who followed him, weren't willing to let Israel forget their past. They reminded the people again and again that they were once slaves. Any spiritual leader who would let them forget that they had been brought "out of the land of Egypt and redeemed . . . from the house of slavery" was speaking treason against the Lord God (Deuteronomy 13:5). Israel was to remember its roots. Once they had been slaves, but God had set them free. Therefore, "You shall have no other gods before me." The commandments begin with an experience. On the basis of that experience, and its memory, God asked for obedience.

The same principle holds for you and me. We Christians reason, on the basis of the New Testament, that we are not under the law of Moses—at least, not in the way Israel was. But we, too, have a past. The Christian faith declares that we were once in the bondage of sin—slaves to sin, to use a biblical term which is meant to be reminiscent of the story of Israel. But we are slaves no longer; we testify that we have been saved. Those who are saved acknowledge that the One who saved them has the right to ask discipleship from them. And the synonym for discipleship is *obedience.*

Unfortunately, many of us don't do very well with this sense of gratitude for our salvation. I have a feeling that members of Alcoholics Anonymous handle their salvation better than most church members do. Perhaps it's because alcoholism carries a more vivid sense of slavery than do our usual problems. Most of us haven't a very strong sense that we were ever lost, or ever in slavery, so we don't get overexcited about being saved. Nor are we likely to become passionate about discipleship. Not unless we realize that there is a magnificent difference between the life we once knew and the life we now live. The Israelites were inclined to forget what Isaiah called "the quarry from which you were dug" (Isaiah 51:1). We have the same problem. In fact, our problem is probably worse.

But if Israel's relationship to the law were only a matter of their having been delivered from slavery and the obligation which they ought therefore to feel, it would be a rather grievous relationship. No matter how well Israel might remember the slavery from which she had been delivered, and no matter how great the sense of gratitude, there would still be an oppressive quality about the law. A feisty soul might complain, "How long does God want me to feel indebted?" Mind you, a saint might not raise such a question, but we aren't all saints. As a matter of fact, as I examine my own soul, I think I might be one of those who would say to God, "Enough about my debt!"

That's where another element enters the story. A *gracious* element. The *covenant.* Israel understood that they were related to God by a contract, an agreement. The Hebrew word for covenant had the root meaning of "bond" or "fetter." This was a binding union, between God and the people of Israel. That, of course, is a quite astonishing idea—that the Lord God of the universe would choose to enter into a contractual agreement with a human body—in this case, a nation.

It is all the more astonishing when we consider the nation in question. Moses is candid when he reminds his people of their ancestry. When bringing their firstfruits to the priest, Moses said, they should say, "A wandering Aramean was my ancestor; he went down into Egypt and lived there as an alien, few in number, and there he became a great nation, mighty and populous" (Deuteronomy 26:5). It's as if Moses were saying, "God could easily have found a better prospect for a covenant—far better than descendants of a wandering Aramean!"

So the covenant was a wonderfully gracious bond. It was by no means a union of equals! Thus, the covenant will have some conditions. The people must expect to keep up their side of the agreement if they are to enjoy its vast benefits. And that's where the commandments come in. Without such a structure of law, the Israelites might well have continued to be "wandering Arameans," a ragtag group of escaped slaves, with nothing to hold them together. As such, they would have been eaten up by the wilderness without their ever reaching the land of promise.

The commandments a hindrance, a frustration? Hardly! They were the essence of life. Without them, Israel would not be a people. The commandments had a wondrous beauty, because they were not only a function of the covenant, but they also were the best assurance that the covenant could be made to work.

It's interesting, and no doubt significant, that the Jews came to celebrate their feast of Pentecost as the time when they were given the Law of Moses. Pentecost was the spring harvest festival. There was a special exuberance about this holiday, because it celebrated the richness and goodness of the earth. For an agrarian world, nothing could mean more than the promise of a good harvest. How remarkable, then, that this festive time came to include the giving of the Law! And yet it makes perfect sense, because the law represented the Covenant. It was Israel's best assurance that they could count on the blessing of God; after all, they were in contract with the Lord.

Pragmatically, they were right—not because some divine magic was on their side, and not because God would send rains and sunshine at the most appropriate times; but because by keeping the Law they were in line with the order of the universe. To break the law was not simply an offense against God; it was an offense against their own best interests. When they violated the law, they destroyed community, they corrupted their relationship with God, and they diminished their own worth.

And yes, because a covenant was involved, they could be equally assured in less prosperous days. One must live with a confidence that goes beyond this year's harvest. If we follow the law, life is on our side. But the benefits are not always immediately obvious. I have known good people, wondrously good people, whose lives never got the recognition or success they seemed to deserve. They have honored the law, but the law hasn't seemed to return the favor. These admirable souls have seen little of what we term success. Other persons, who have seemed to acknowledge the law only when they found it convenient, have nevertheless prospered.

Then, more than ever, one had better be assured that the law is right, and that the covenant is sure. Such confidence is more important in the times of failing harvest than in the days of abundance. Sometimes we must have a divine doggedness about what is right. Do some steal and by their cleverness not get caught? No matter. Are some adulterous, and sleep soundly at night? No matter. Do some treat God as an adjunct, yet go blithely on? No matter. The law still stands, and the

Covenant is sure. Indeed, the law stands *because* it is part of the Covenant.

The late Bishop Gerald Kennedy spoke often of a picture which hung on the office wall of a good friend. He had looked at it once and could never forget it. It portrayed two elderly Jewish men who were fleeing from a burning city. Apparently a pogrom had broken out, and they were running for their very lives. But in their arms they had a scroll of the Law. They would preserve this even if it meant leaving all their other possessions. They would sacrifice their lives for their scroll of the Law.

We Christians cling instead to the cross, and with good and eternal reason. But that shouldn't diminish our regard for the value of the law. The law was also God's gift. And though it could not provide salvation, it did offer a new quality of life to those who would honor it.

The law is much more than a set of rules. It is God's outline for effective living. In a world where sin and stupidity so often write a great *no* across our lives, the Ten Commandments offer a grand *yes*. If I were nothing but a secular pragmatist, wanting only to save my own skin and to live somewhat effectively, I would obey the ten commandments. Good sense would tell me to do so.

As a Christian, I have a better reason by far; I obey these commandments because I love God. And loving God, I have found that these laws are an expression of divine love for our human race. They are God's grand answer to all that is negative and destructive. They are God's loving *Yes*.

SUGGESTIONS FOR LEADING A STUDY OF *THE TEN COMMANDMENTS FROM THE BACK SIDE*

John D. Schroeder

*T*he Ten Commandments from the Back Side *is a collection of essays designed to stimulate our thinking about the Ten Commandments. This study guide is intended to assist you in facilitating a discussion group, so that the experience is beneficial for both you and your group. Here are some thoughts on how you can help your group:*

1. Distribute the book to participants before your first group meeting and request that they come having read the introduction. You may want to limit the size of your group to increase participation.

2. Participants may ask what the title of the book means. The "back side" means simply a different perspective in order to gain new insights about ourselves, others, and our faith.

3. Begin your sessions on time. Your participants will appreciate your promptness. You may want to begin your first session with introductions and a brief get-acquainted time. Start each session by reading aloud the snapshot summary of the chapter for the day.

4. Select discussion questions and activities in advance. Note that the first question is usually a general question designed to get discussion going. Feel free to change the order of the listed questions and create your own questions. Allow a set amount of time for the questions and activities.

5. Remind your participants that all questions are valid as part of the learning process. Encourage their participation in discussion by saying there are no "wrong" answers and that all input will be appreciated. Invite them to share their thoughts, personal stories, and ideas as their comfort level dictates.

6. Some questions may be more difficult to answer than others. If you ask a question and no one responds, begin the discussion by venturing an answer yourself. Then ask for comments and other answers. Remember that some questions may have multiple answers.

7. Ask the question "Why?" or "Why do you believe that?" to help continue a discussion and give it greater depth.

8. Give everyone a chance to talk. Keep the conversation moving. Occasionally you may want to direct a question at a specific person who has been quiet. "Do you have anything to add?" is a good follow-up question to another person. If the topic of conversation gets off track, move ahead by asking the next question.

9. Before moving from questions to activities, ask members if they have any questions that have not been answered. Remember that as a leader, you do not have to know all the answers. Some answers may come from group members. Other answers may even need a bit of research. Your job is to keep the discussion moving and to encourage participation.

10. Review the activity in advance. Feel free to modify it or create your own activity. Encourage participants to try the home activity.

11. Following the conclusion of the activity, close with a brief prayer; either the printed prayer or one of your own. If your group desires, pause for individual prayer petitions.

12. Be grateful and supportive. Thank members for their ideas and participation.

13. You are not expected to be a "perfect" leader. Just do the best you can by focusing on the participants and lesson. God will help you lead this group.

14. Enjoy your time together.

Suggestions for Participants

1. What you receive from this study is in direct proportion to your involvement. Be an active participant.

2. Please make a point to attend all sessions and to arrive on time so you receive the greatest benefit.

3. Read the lesson and review the questions prior to the meeting. You may want to jot down questions you have from the reading and also answers to some of the study guide questions.

4. Be supportive and appreciative of your group leader as well as the other members of the group. You are on a journey together.

5. Your participation is encouraged. Feel free to share your thoughts about the material being discussed.

6. Pray for your group and your leader.

Introduction: The No That Gives Us *Yes*

Snapshot Summary

This book looks at the Ten Commandments from the "back side." The "back side" means simply a different or fresh perspective in order to gain insights about our faith. This introduction looks at how people view the Law and how the Law acts as a friend.

Discussion Questions

1. What insights did you receive from this introduction?
2. What are your first memories of the Ten Commandments?
3. Recall an early experience of being told "no."
4. Recall an early experience of being told "yes."
5. What is your definition of a friend?
6. Name an object that you consider a friend.

7. What thoughts come to mind when you hear the word "law"?
8. What laws did you learn early in life?
9. How is God's law different from human law?
10. Recall an early life lesson in the difference between right and wrong.

Activities

As a group: Share what you hope to receive from this study.

At home: Tell someone you are in a group studying the Ten Commandments. See how they respond.

Prayer: Dear God, we thank you that in your perfect love you have given us the Law. May your Law continue to bless us and others as we grow closer to you. Amen.

CHAPTER 1

To Begin at the Beginning

EXODUS 20:3

Snapshot Summary

This first chapter deals with the issue of priorities in life and how they relate to the first commandment.

Discussion Questions

1. What insights did you receive from this chapter?
2. What are some common priorities?
3. What priorities are the easiest? the toughest?
4. Next to God, what are some of your other priorities?
5. What are some of your lowest priorities?
6. Why do the commandments begin with God?
7. What is the benefit of making God first in our life?
8. What are the consequences of not putting God first?

9. Of what does the first commandment remind us, by inference?
10. How is life "frittered away"?

Activities

As a group: Brainstorm actions and ideas to keep God a priority.

At home: Try to carry out one idea from your group's list.

Prayer: Jesus, help us to put you first and to look to you to keep our priorities straight. Thank you for making us your priority. Amen.

CHAPTER 2

Believing Is More Than Seeing

EXODUS 20:4

Snapshot Summary

This chapter looks at idols that come between us and God.

Discussion Questions

1. What insights did you receive from this chapter?
2. Name some idols common in our world today.
3. Explain how this commandment relates to our perception of God.
4. What are the traits or ingredients of idols?
5. What is the appeal of an idol?
6. Why are idols so dangerous?
7. What is the purpose of the second commandment?
8. What do we learn of God's love from this commandment?

9. In what ways do we restrict God?
10. Recall any idols that you struggled with as a child.

Activities:

As a group: Look at magazine ads to locate products that promise success and status. Discuss idols that are promoted in ads.

At home: Meditate on and identify the idols in your life. Focus on eliminating them.

Prayer: Loving Father, no words or illustrations can capture you or your love for us. You are beyond images. Forgive us for restricting you and trying to use you to meet our selfish needs. Amen.

CHAPTER 3

Living in the Name

EXODUS 20:7

Snapshot Summary

This chapter explores the proper use of God's name and the importance of names.

Discussion Questions

1. What insights did you receive from this chapter?
2. Why are names important?
3. Do you know the meaning of your name? Share it with the group.
4. How do you feel when someone calls you by the wrong name?
5. Why are we sometimes not respectful of the names of others?
6. Discuss how names can be powerful.

7. Why did God give us this commandment?
8. How does this commandment go beyond swearing?
9. What is the danger in becoming too casual with the use of God's name?
10. What are ways we can live in the power of God's name?

Activities

As a group: Use a Bible to locate and list the many names of God. Discuss their different meanings.

At home: Ask several people the origin of their names. Be conscious of names this week.

Prayer: Dear God, we thank you that you have called us by name. Help us to use your name properly, with respect and honor. May we live in the power of your name. Amen.

CHAPTER 4

The Gift of Rest

EXODUS 20:8-10*a*

Snapshot Summary

This chapter helps us understand the sabbath day and use it as the gift God intended.

Discussion Questions

1. What insights did you receive from this chapter?
2. Why do you think the sabbath is misunderstood? Explain.
3. Why did God give us the gift of the sabbath?
4. How does God want us to use this gift?
5. How do you think our observance of the sabbath today differs from fifty years ago?

6. What are the benefits of pausing from our routines for a day?
7. How does the sabbath deliver us from slavery?
8. How does the sabbath demonstrate holiness of time?
9. Discuss: The proper response to a gift is to love it.
10. What gets in our way of honoring the sabbath?

Activities

As a group: Share some of your childhood memories of Sundays.

At home: Think of a way to make the next sabbath special and report to the group next week what you did.

Prayer: Dear Lord, we thank you for your gift of the sabbath. Help us to treasure it and respond to your gift with love and acceptance. Amen.

CHAPTER 5

Futures Unlimited

EXODUS 20:12

Snapshot Summary

This chapter helps us explore our relationship with our parents and the issue of honor.

Discussion Questions

1. What insights did you receive from this chapter?
2. Recall some early memories of your parents.
3. Discuss the meaning of the word "honor."
4. How are the past and the future connected in this commandment?
5. What are the results when parents are not honored?

6. How does the chapter expand the definition of "parents"?
7. Why did God give us this commandment?
8. What actions do we need to take in order to honor someone?
9. What motivates us to honor?
10. How do "blessing" and "honor" fit together?

Activities

As a group: Visit a nursing home together.

At home: Create your own "Honor Your Parents Week." Activities could include writing a letter, visiting a cemetery, or helping children value the gift of parents.

Prayer: God, we thank you for our parents and for being our heavenly parent. Help us to honor our parents and to be thankful for all their sacrifices. Amen.

CHAPTER 6

Part of the Mainland

EXODUS 20:13

Snapshot Summary

This chapter examines the issue of murder in thought, word, and deed.

Discussion Questions

1. What insights did you receive from this chapter?
2. How does the world cheapen human life? How do we sometimes participate?
3. What makes people so important to God? to us? to others?
4. What do anger and murder have in common?

5. What are some ways that we can embrace life?
6. What causes people to murder?
7. What causes people to love others?
8. Recall a time that you witnessed a "murder."
9. How can we all be "part of the mainland"?
10. Discuss: "One can't inflict death without in some measure dying."

Activities

As a group: Recall acts of kindness—people who affirmed you and embraced life.

At home: Go out of your way to affirm someone and be kind. Kill someone with kindness. Report results back to the group.

Prayer: Dear Lord, we thank you for your precious gift of life. Help us to value it always and embrace life in our daily activities. Amen.

CHAPTER 7

Redeeming the Sacred

EXODUS 20:14

Snapshot Summary

This chapter examines the issue of adultery and its many ramifications.

Discussion Questions

1. What insights did you receive from this chapter?
2. What are some of the causes of adultery?
3. What are some of the consequences of adultery?
4. How does adultery hurt our nation?

5. Give a definition of adultery. Have others add to it.
6. What makes adultery so complicated?
7. What messages do we get from our society about adultery?
8. How do marriages benefit when partners abstain from adultery?
9. What are some ways to avoid adultery when tempted?
10. What should our response be to someone who has committed adultery?

Activities

As a group: Read and discuss Deuteronomy 22:22-27.

At home: Pray for those tempted with adultery.

Prayer: Dear Lord, we cherish our relationship with you. Help us to value faithfulness and commitment to each other and to you. Amen.

CHAPTER 8

To Each His Own

EXODUS 20:15

Snapshot Summary

This chapter explores the issue of stealing, the costs involved, and the importance of property.

Discussion Questions

1. What insights did you receive from this chapter?
2. Recall a time during your childhood when you took something.
3. Discuss the costs of stealing to our society.
4. Do you think stealing is worse now than in the past? explain.
5. What is meant by "stealing from life"?

6. Why is it better to be the victim of theft rather than the one who steals?
7. How have you felt as a victim of theft?
8. What are the personal consequences of stealing?
9. Why is property important?
10. What can make it easy to steal?

Activities

As a group: List and discuss different types of stealing.

At home: Put into practice some ways you can make your neighborhood safer.

Prayer: Dear Lord, thank you for what you have given us. Help us to be content with what we have and respect and protect the property of others. Amen.

CHAPTER 9

Blessed Communicators

EXODUS 20:16

Snapshot Summary

This chapter focuses on accurate communication and how we serve God and others by telling the truth.

Discussion Questions

1. What insights did you receive from this chapter?
2. What motivates us sometimes to be a false witness?
3. Discuss the many forms of being a false witness.
4. When are we most tempted to lie?
5. How long does a lie or untrue statement live?
6. Have you ever been hurt by a false witness? Share your story.

7. How can we avoid being a false witness?
8. How can inappropriate silence be just as damaging as telling a lie?
9. What damage do you cause to yourself when you lie? to others?
10. Why is the listener sometimes as guilty as the talker?

Activities

As a group: Discuss how it would feel to be accused of a crime you did not commit, because of a false witness.

At home: Make an effort to correct one untruth you hear during the week. Strive to speak the truth.

Prayer: Dear God, you have given us words so that we may praise you and affirm others. Thank you for your gift of communication. May we use words wisely and always speak the truth. Amen.

CHAPTER 10

A Matter of Vision

EXODUS 20:17

Snapshot Summary

In this chapter we explore the secret sin of coveting and how it damages our relationship with God and others.

Discussion Questions

1. What insights did you receive from this chapter?
2. What motivates us to covet?
3. What objects are most tempting to covet? Does their value always matter?
4. When we covet, what happens to our relationship with God?

5. How can we gain a spirit of contentment?
6. Why are the first and tenth commandments "bookends"?
7. How does coveting affect our relationship with others?
8. How does coveting distort our values?
9. What is the irony of covetousness?
10. Why does the author say that covetousness is almost always nearsighted?

Activities

As a group: Give each person a different-color crayon. Share your reasons why someone else's color is best.

At home: Reflect on your own issues concerning coveting.

Prayer: Dear Lord, thank you for all our possessions. Help us to appreciate what is ours and not desire the property of others. Amen.

EPILOGUE

A Privileged People

Snapshot Summary

In this epilogue we look at the Ten Commandments as a whole along with some historical background.

Discussion Questions

1. What insights did you receive from reading this epilogue?
2. On what grounds does God ask for our obedience?
3. What is our "past" of slavery as Christians? explain.
4. What is the Covenant?
5. How are the commandments the product of a relationship?
6. How do you now see the Ten Commandments as a friend?
7. What new information about Jewish history did you learn from reading this book?

8. Share with the group a new perspective on one of the commandments you gained from this book.
9. What is the relationship between the Law and the Covenant?
10. How are the Ten Commandments God's outline for effective living?

Activities

As a group: Discuss how you view the Ten Commandments differently now.

At home: Read Exodus 20 and meditate on what the Ten Commandments mean to you.

Prayer: God, we praise you for your gift of the Ten Commandments. Thank you for giving us this time together to learn more about you and ourselves. Be with us as we go our separate ways and continue to encourage us with your love. Amen.